Smart Internet of Things Projects

Discover how to build your own smart Internet of Things projects and bring a new degree of interconnectivity to your world

Agus Kurniawan

BIRMINGHAM - MUMBAI

Smart Internet of Things Projects

First published: September 2016

Production reference: 1280916

Published by Packt Publishing Ltd.
Livery Place
35 Livery Street
Birmingham B3 2PB, UK.

ISBN 978-1-78646-651-8

www.packtpub.com

Credits

Author
Agus Kurniawan

Reviewer
Phodal Huang

Acquisition Editor
Rahul Nair

Content Development Editor
Trusha Shriyan

Technical Editor
Nirant Carvalho

Copy Editor
Safis Editing

Project Coordinator
Kinjal Bari

Proofreader
Safis Editing

Indexer
Pratik Shirodkar

Graphics
Kirk D'Penha

Production Coordinator
Shantanu N. Zagade

Cover Work
Shantanu N. Zagade

About the Author

Agus Kurniawan is a lecturer, IT consultant, and an author. He has 14 years of experience in various software and hardware development projects, delivering materials in training and workshops, and technical writing. He has been awarded the Microsoft Most Valuable Professional (MVP) award 12 years in a row.

He is currently doing some research and also getting involved in teaching activities related to networking and security systems at the Faculty of Computer Science, Universitas Indonesia and Samsung R&D Institute, Indonesia. Currently, he is pursuing a PhD in computer science at the Freie Universität Berlin, Germany. He can be reached on his blog at `http://blog.aguskurniawan.net` and Twitter at `@agusk2010`.

About the Reviewer

Phodal Huang has over six years' experience in hardware development & web development. He was graduated from Xi'an University of Arts & Science. He currently works at ThoughtWorks as a Consultant. He is owner of the mini IoT project (`https://github.com/phodal/iot`), author of the E-book Design IoT (`http://designiot.phodal.com`, Chinese only). He is also the reviewer of *Learning Internet of Things*. Author of *Design Internet of Things* which was wrote in Chinese, and now in publishing process.

He loves designing, writing, hacking, you can find out more about him on his personal website at `http://www.phodal.com`. He also love open source software development, you can also find out more information at `http://github.com/phodal`.

www.PacktPub.com

eBooks, discount offers, and more

Did you know that Packt offers eBook versions of every book published, with PDF and ePub files available? You can upgrade to the eBook version at www.PacktPub.com and as a print book customer, you are entitled to a discount on the eBook copy. Get in touch with us at customercare@packtpub.com for more details.

At www.PacktPub.com, you can also read a collection of free technical articles, sign up for a range of free newsletters and receive exclusive discounts and offers on Packt books and eBooks.

https://www.packtpub.com/mapt

Get the most in-demand software skills with Mapt. Mapt gives you full access to all Packt books and video courses, as well as industry-leading tools to help you plan your personal development and advance your career.

Why subscribe?

- Fully searchable across every book published by Packt
- Copy and paste, print, and bookmark content
- On demand and accessible via a web browser

Table of Contents

Preface

Internet of Things is a groundbreaking technology that is connecting numerous physical devices to the internet and controlling them. Creating basic IoT projects is common but imagine building smart IoT projects that can extract data from physical devices, thereby making decision by itself.

Smart Internet of Things project is an essential reference of practical solution to build a project that combines IoT and intelligent system. Basic statistics and various applied algorithms on Data Science and Machine Learning are introduced to accelerate your learning of how to integrate decision system into the physical devices. This book contains IoT projects, such as building a smart temperature controller, creating your own vision machine project, how to build an autonomous mobile robot like a car, how to control IoT projects through voice command, building IoT applications utilizing cloud technology, and data science and many more.

I hope you find this book useful and that it will help you to take your skill to a higher level.

What this book covers

Chapter 1, *Make Your IoT Project Smart*, helps you to sense and actuate from IoT devices, such as Arduino and Raspberry Pi. Various Python libraries related to Statistics and Data Science is introduced so that we know their existence.

Chapter 2, *Decision System for IoT Projects*, helps you learn how to build a decision system that is implemented on IoT devices. Reviewing some Python libraries related to decision system and then implementing decision system program into IoT boards will also be covered.

Chapter 3, Build Your Own Machine Vision, explores how to make a machine to see by deploying a camera and starting to understand machine vision till we detect and track object model by training our machine. Several camera modules will also be reviewed.

Chapter 4, Make Your Own Autonomous Car Robot, explores how to build a car robot. It integrates some sensor and actuator devices to make a robot run without human interference. We will also learn how to navigate a robot and control it from your computer.

Chapter 5, Building Voice Technology on IoT Projects, helps you in making your IoT board speak something. Various sound and speech modules will be explored during the project journey.

Chapter 6, Building Data Science-based Cloud for IoT Projects, explores how to apply cloud platforms on IoT projects; back-end infrastructure for our IoT projects is also important. By distributing IoT boards on some locations with different countries needs more attention in acquiring sensor data.

What you need for this book

You should have Raspberry Pi, Arduino and several electronics components to run the entire projects in this book.

Who this book is for

This book is for those who want to learn how to build IoT projects with integrating various machine learning algorithms. You also will learn to implement machine learning into IoT project in real application. However, you don't need to have any previous experience with the Raspberry Pi and Arduino.

Conventions

In this book, you will find a number of text styles that distinguish between different kinds of information. Here are some examples of these styles and an explanation of their meaning.

Code words in text, database table names, folder names, filenames, file extensions, pathnames, dummy URLs, user input, and Twitter handles are shown as follows: " We build a linear regression using sm.OLS()."

A block of code is set as follows:

```
import RPi.GPIO as GPIO
import time

led_pin = 17
GPIO.setmode(GPIO.BCM)
GPIO.setup(led_pin, GPIO.OUT)
```

When we wish to draw your attention to a particular part of a code block, the relevant lines or items are set in bold:

```
try:
    while 1:
        print("turn on led")
        GPIO.output(led_pin, GPIO.HIGH)
        time.sleep(2)
        print("turn off led")
        GPIO.output(led_pin, GPIO.LOW)
        time.sleep(2)

except KeyboardInterrupt:
    GPIO.output(led_pin, GPIO.LOW)
    GPIO.cleanup()

print("done")
```

Any command-line input or output is written as follows:

```
$ mkdirgps_web
$ cdgps_web
$ nano gspapp.py
```

New terms and **important words** are shown in bold. Words that you see on the screen, for example, in menus or dialog boxes, appear in the text like this: "Click the menu **Sketch | Include Library | Manage Libraries** so you will get a dialog."

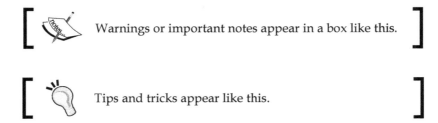

> Warnings or important notes appear in a box like this.

> Tips and tricks appear like this.

Reader feedback

Feedback from our readers is always welcome. Let us know what you think about this book—what you liked or disliked. Reader feedback is important for us as it helps us develop titles that you will really get the most out of.

To send us general feedback, simply e-mail feedback@packtpub.com, and mention the book's title in the subject of your message.

If there is a topic that you have expertise in and you are interested in either writing or contributing to a book, see our author guide at www.packtpub.com/authors.

Customer support

Now that you are the proud owner of a Packt book, we have a number of things to help you to get the most from your purchase.

Downloading the example code

You can download the example code files for this book from your account at http://www.packtpub.com. If you purchased this book elsewhere, you can visit http://www.packtpub.com/support and register to have the files e-mailed directly to you.

You can download the code files by following these steps:

1. Log in or register to our website using your e-mail address and password.
2. Hover the mouse pointer on the **SUPPORT** tab at the top.
3. Click on **Code Downloads & Errata**.
4. Enter the name of the book in the **Search** box.
5. Select the book for which you're looking to download the code files.
6. Choose from the drop-down menu where you purchased this book from.
7. Click on **Code Download**.

You can also download the code files by clicking on the **Code Files** button on the book's webpage at the Packt Publishing website. This page can be accessed by entering the book's name in the **Search** box. Please note that you need to be logged in to your Packt account.

Once the file is downloaded, please make sure that you unzip or extract the folder using the latest version of:

* WinRAR / 7-Zip for Windows
* Zipeg / iZip / UnRarX for Mac
* 7-Zip / PeaZip for Linux

The code bundle for the book is also hosted on GitHub at `https://github.com/PacktPublishing/Smart-Internet-of-Things-Projects`. We also have other code bundles from our rich catalog of books and videos available at `https://github.com/PacktPublishing/`. Check them out!

Errata

Although we have taken every care to ensure the accuracy of our content, mistakes do happen. If you find a mistake in one of our books—maybe a mistake in the text or the code—we would be grateful if you could report this to us. By doing so, you can save other readers from frustration and help us improve subsequent versions of this book. If you find any errata, please report them by visiting `http://www.packtpub.com/submit-errata`, selecting your book, clicking on the **Errata Submission Form** link, and entering the details of your errata. Once your errata are verified, your submission will be accepted and the errata will be uploaded to our website or added to any list of existing errata under the Errata section of that title.

To view the previously submitted errata, go to https://www.packtpub.com/books/content/support and enter the name of the book in the search field. The required information will appear under the **Errata** section.

Piracy

Piracy of copyrighted material on the Internet is an ongoing problem across all media. At Packt, we take the protection of our copyright and licenses very seriously. If you come across any illegal copies of our works in any form on the Internet, please provide us with the location address or website name immediately so that we can pursue a remedy.

Please contact us at copyright@packtpub.com with a link to the suspected pirated material.

We appreciate your help in protecting our authors and our ability to bring you valuable content.

Questions

If you have a problem with any aspect of this book, you can contact us at questions@packtpub.com, and we will do our best to address the problem.

1
Making Your IoT Project Smart

We're going to begin by reviewing basic statistics. Then we will learn how to sense and actuate from **Internet of Things (IoT)** devices such as Arduino and Raspberry Pi. We will also introduce various Python libraries related to statistics and data. These libraries are useful for building our project throughout this book.

By the end of this chapter, you'll have learned about the following:

- Introducing basic statistics and data science
- Reviewing several IoT devices and platforms
- Sensing and actuating through external devices on IoT devices
- Building a smart IoT project

Let's get started!

Introducing basic statistics and data science

Let's say you want to know the temperature of your room, so you measure it every hour during the day using a particular tool. This data is necessary because you want to decide whether to buy an **AC (Air Conditioning)** machine or not. After measurement is done, you obtain a list of temperature data. The results of your measurements can be seen in the following table:

Time	Temperature (Celsius)	Time	Temperature (Celsius)
01:00	18	13:00	28
02:00	17	14:00	29
03:00	18	15:00	28
04:00	19	16:00	27
05:00	20	17:00	25
06:00	20	18:00	24
07:00	21	19:00	24
08:00	22	20:00	23
09:00	22	21:00	22
10:00	24	22:00	20
11:00	25	23:00	19
12:00	26	24:00	19

The preceding table shows of the temperature data in tabular form. You try to understand the meaning of the data. For this situation, you need some knowledge of statistics, along with some statistics terms such as mean, median, variance, and standard deviation.

Suppose we have a sample of *n* data, which is designated by *x1, x2, x3, ..., xn*. We can calculate mean, median, variance, and standard deviation using the following formulas:

$$mean = \bar{x} = \frac{\sum_{i=1}^{n} x_i}{n}$$

$$median = value\ on\ position\frac{n+1}{2}, if\ n\ is\ odd$$

$$median = value\ on\ position\ between\ n/2\ and\ (n/2)+1, if\ n\ is\ even$$

$$variance = s^2 = \frac{\sum_{i=1}^{n}(x_i - \bar{x})^2}{n-1}$$

$$Standard\ deviation = s = \sqrt{\frac{\sum_{i=1}^{n}(x_i - \bar{x})^2}{n-1}}$$

 To compute median value, you should arrange the data in ascending order.

From the preceding table, you can calculate the mean, median, variance and standard deviation using the preceding formulas. You should obtain values of 22.5, 22, 12.348, and 3.514 respectively.

To understand the pattern of the data, you try to visualize it in graphics form, for instance, using Microsoft Excel. The result can be seen in the following figure:

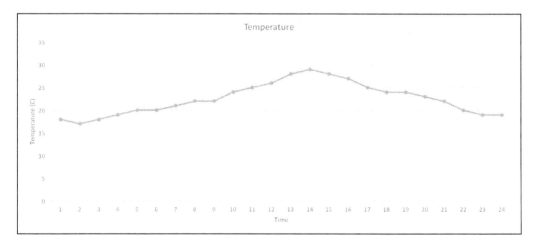

You can see that the average temperature of your room is 22.5 Celsius. The temperature maximum and minimum values are 19 and 17, respectively. With this information, you can think about what type of AC machine you want to buy.

Furthermore, you can extend your investigation by measuring your room's temperature for a week. After you have measured, you can plot the measurements in graphics form, for instance, using Microsoft Excel. A sample of temperature measurements is shown in the following figure:

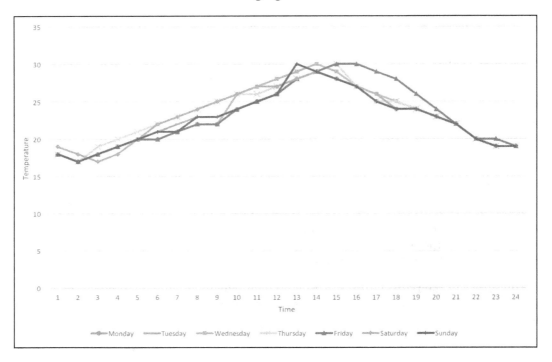

The graph shows room temperature changes every day. If you measure it every day for a year, you should see temperature trends in your room. Knowledge of data science can improve your ability to learn from data. Of course, some statistics and machine learning computing are involved to get insight how data behaviors are.

This book will help you to get started with how to apply data science and machine learning in real cases, with a focus on IoT fields.

Python for computational statistics and data science

Python is a widely used, general purpose programming language. Starting to program with Python is a good point. Python provides simple programming syntax and a lot of APIs, which we can use to expand our program.

To use Python on your computer, you can download and install it from `https://www.python.org/downloads/` if your OS does not yet have it installed. After completing the installation, we can run the Python program via Terminal, or the Command Prompt on the Windows platform, by typing the following command:

```
$ python
```

 Note: remove $ sign. Just type `python` on Terminal. This is applicable to Python 2.x.

Once you have executed the command, you should see the Python command prompt, as shown in the following screenshot:

```
agusk$ python
Python 2.7.10 (default, Oct 23 2015, 19:19:21)
[GCC 4.2.1 Compatible Apple LLVM 7.0.0 (clang-700.0.59.5)] on darwin
Type "help", "copyright", "credits" or "license" for more information.
>>>
```

If you installed Python 3, you usually run the program using the following command:

```
$ python3
```

You should see the Python 3 shell on your Terminal:

```
agusk — Python — 80×23

agusk$ python3
Python 3.5.1 (default, Jan 22 2016, 08:54:32)
[GCC 4.2.1 Compatible Apple LLVM 7.0.2 (clang-700.1.81)] on darwin
Type "help", "copyright", "credits" or "license" for more information.
>>>
```

What's next?

There are lots of Python resources to help you learn how to write programs using Python. I recommend to reading the Python documents at https://www.python. org/doc/. You can also read Python books to accelerate your learning. This book does not cover topics about the basic Python programming language.

Python libraries for computational statistics and data science

Python has big communities. They help their members to learn and share. Several community members have been open sources related to computational statistics and data science, which can be used for our work. We will use these libraries for our implementation.

The following are several Python libraries for statistics and data science.

NumPy

NumPy is a fundamental package for efficient scientific computing in Python. This library has capabilities for handling N-dimensional arrays and integrating C/C++ and Fortran code. It also provides features for linear algebra, Fourier transform, and random number.

The official website for NumPy can be found at `http://www.numpy.org`.

Pandas

Pandas is a library for handling table-like structures called **DataFrame** objects. This has powerful and efficient numerical operations similar to NumPy's array object.

Further information about pandas can be found at `http://pandas.pydata.org`.

SciPy

SciPy is an expansion of the NumPy library. It contains functions for linear algebra, interpolation, integration, clustering, and so on.

The official website can be found at `http://scipy.org/scipylib/index.html`.

Scikit-learn

Scikit-learn is the most popular machine learning library for Python. It provides many functionalities, such as preprocessing data, classification, regression, clustering, dimensionality reduction, and model selection.

Further information about Scikit-learn can be found at `http://scikit-learn.org/stable/`.

Shogun

Shogun is a machine learning library for Python, which focuses on large-scale kernel methods such as **support vector machines** (**SVMs**). This library comes with a range of different SVM implementations.

The official website can be found at `http://www.shogun-toolbox.org`.

SymPy

SymPy is a Python library for symbolic mathematical computations. It has capabilities in calculus, algebra, geometry, discrete mathematics, quantum physics, and more.

The official website can be found at `http://www.sympygamma.com`.

Statsmodels

Statsmodels is a Python module we can use to process data, estimate statistical models and test data.

You can find out more about Statsmodels by visiting the official website at `http://statsmodels.sourceforge.net`.

Building a simple program for statistics

In the first section, you already measure room temperature. Now we will try to perform some simple computational statistics using Statsmodels. We will use our measurement results data and then build a linear regression for our data.

First, we should install Statsmodels. This library needs required libraries such as NumPy, SciPy, pandas, and patsy. We can install them using `pip`. Type the following command:

```
$ pip install numpy scipy pandas patsy statsmodels
```

If you get a problem related to security access, you can run this command using `sudo`:

```
$ sudo pip install numpy scipy pandas patsy statsmodels
```

If your computer doesn't have `pip` installed, you can install it by following the guidelines at `https://pip.pypa.io/en/stable/installing/`.

For testing, we create a Python program. Write the following scripts:

```
import numpy as np
import statsmodels.api as sm

# room temperature
Y = [18, 17, 18, 19, 20, 20, 21, 22, 22, 24, 25, 26, 28, 29, 28, 27,
25, 24, 24, 23, 22, 20, 19, 19]
X = range(1, 25)
```

```
X = sm.add_constant(X)

model = sm.OLS(Y, X)
results = model.fit()

# print
print(results.params)
print(results.tvalues)


print(results.t_test([1, 0]))
print(results.f_test(np.identity(2)))
```

We build a linear regression using `sm.OLS()`. We then do estimation using `model.fit()`. Finally, we print the computation result. Save the program in a file called `ch01_linear.py`.

Now you can run this program using the following command:

$ python ch01_linear.py

If you have installed Python 3, you can run this program using the following command:

$ python3 ch01_linear.py

You should see the program output shown in the following screenshot. I run this program using Python 3:

```
● ● ●                      codes — -bash — 80×18
agusk$ python3 ch01_linear.py
[ 20.43478261    0.16521739]
[ 14.31244119    1.65345307]
                         Test for Constraints
==============================================================================
                coef     std err          t      P>|t|     [95.0% Conf. Int.]
------------------------------------------------------------------------------
c0             20.4348     1.428     14.312      0.000      17.474     23.396
==============================================================================
<F test: F=array([[ 530.44612737]]), p=2.4333902675836626e-19, df_denom=22, df_n
um=2>
agusk$ 
```

IoT devices and platforms

The IoT platform has the capability to connect to an Internet network and interact with other platforms. Generally speaking, talking about IoT in terms of device platform is a huge topic. In this section, we will explore several IoT device platforms that are widely used in client side.

Arduino

Arduino is a widely used development board. This board is well known in the embedded community. Most Arduino boards are built using Atmel AVR, but some boards use other MCUs regarding to who joints venture with Arduino. Currently, Arduino boards are built by Arduino.cc and Arduino.org. Other companies also build boards, which are usually called Arduino-compatible. This is because the founder of Arduino already shared the board scheme so that people can build own Arduino. Please make sure you use a board and software from the same company.

To extend Arduino I/O and functionalities, we can use Arduino shields. There are many Arduino shields, with different purposes, for instance, Bluetooth, Wi-Fi, GSM, temperature, and humidity sensors. The benefit of using the Arduino shield is that it allows you to focus on board development. We just have to attach Arduino shield to the Arduino board without any soldering.

We're going to review several Arduino boards from Arduino.cc. We can read a comparison of all Arduino boards from Arduino.cc by visiting this site: http://www.arduino.cc/en/Products/Compare. We will review Arduino boards such as Arduino Uno, Arduino 101, and Arduino MKR1000.

The Arduino Uno model is widely used in Arduino development. It's built on top of a MCU ATmega328P microcontroller. The board provides several digital and analog I/O pins, to which we can attach our sensor and actuator devices. SPI and I2C protocols are also provided by the Arduino Uno. For further information about the board, I recommend you read the board specification at http://www.arduino.cc/en/Main/ArduinoBoardUno. You can see an Arduino Uno board in the following figure:

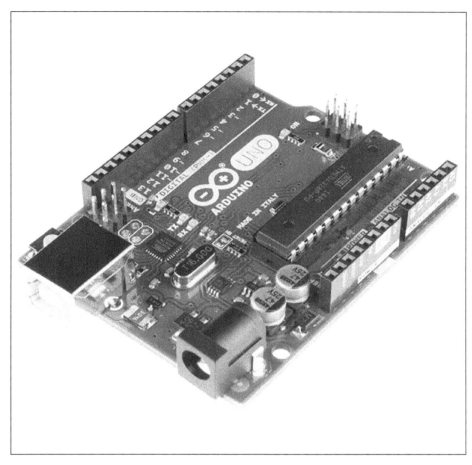

Source: https://www.sparkfun.com/products/11021

Arduino 101 is the same as Arduino Uno in terms of I/O pins. Arduino 101 runs Intel Curie, http://www.intel.com/content/www/us/en/wearables/wearable-soc.html, as its core module. This board has a built-in Bluetooth module. If you want your Arduino 101 connect to a Wi-Fi network, you should add an additional Wi-Fi shield. I recommend you use Arduino Wi-Fi Shield 101, http://www.arduino.cc/en/Main/ArduinoWiFiShield101.

The following figure shows an Arduino 101 board:

Source: https://www.sparkfun.com/products/13850

Arduino MKR1000 is a new board at the time of writing. This board uses the Atmel ATSAMW25 SoC, which provides a built-in Wi-Fi module. I recommend using this board as an IoT solution for the Arduino platform because the Wi-Fi module, WINC1500, is supported for SSL and ECC508 CryptoAuthentication. Further information about this board can be found at http://www.arduino.cc/en/Main/ArduinoMKR1000.

The following figure shows the Arduino MKR1000 board:

Source: http://www.arduino.cc/en/Main/ArduinoMKR1000

Raspberry Pi

The Raspberry Pi is a low-cost with credit card-sized computer created by Eben Upton. It's a mini computer for educational purposes. To see all Raspberry Pi models, you can go to https://www.raspberrypi.org/products/. You can see Raspberry Pi 3 Model B and Raspberry Pi Zero in the following explanation.

The Raspberry Pi 3 Model B is the third generation of Raspberry Pi. This board consists of a Quad-Core 64-bit CPU, Wi-Fi, and Bluetooth. It's highly recommended for your IoT solution.

The following figure shows a Raspberry Pi 3 Model B board:

Source: `https://thepihut.com/collections/raspberry-pi/products/`
`raspberry-pi-3-model-b`

The Raspberry Pi Zero is a small computer half the size of the Model A+. It runs with a single-core CPU and no network module, but it provides a micro HDMI to be connected to a monitor. Due to the lack of network module, you will need an extended module, for instance, Ethernet USB or Wi-Fi USB, to connect Raspberry Pi Zero to a network.

The following image shows a Raspberry Pi Zero board:

Source: https://thepihut.com/collections/raspberry-pi-zero/products/raspberry-pi-zero

BeagleBone Black and Green

BeagleBone Black (BBB) Rev C is a development kit based on an AM335x processor, which integrates an ARM Cortex™-A8 core operating at up to 1 GHz. BBB is more powerful than Raspberry Pi. A BBB board also provides internal 4 GB 8-bit eMMC on-board flash storage.

BBB supports several OSes such as Debian, Android, and Ubuntu. To find out more about BBB, go to https://beagleboard.org/black.

The following figure shows a BeagleBone Black board:

Source: http://www.exp-tech.de/beaglebone-black-rev-c-element14

 SeeedStudio **BeagleBone Green** (**BBG**) is a joint effort by BeagleBoard.org and Seeed Studio. BBG has the same features as the BBB, except the HDMI port is replaced by Grove connectors, so the BBG's price is lower than the BBB. You can review and buy this board at http://www.seeedstudio.com/depot/SeeedStudio-BeagleBone-Green-p-2504.html.

The following figure shows a BBG board:

Source: http://www.seeedstudio.com/depot/SeeedStudio-BeagleBone-Green-p-2504.html

IoT boards based on ESP8266 MCU?

The ESP8266 is a low-cost Wi-Fi MCU with integrated TCP/IP. It's built by Espressif Systems, a Chinese manufacturer. You can find further information about this chip at http://espressif.com/en/products/hardware/esp8266ex/overview.

There are many boards based on the ESP8266 chip. The following is a list of board platforms that are built on top of an ESP8266 MCU:

- **NodeMCU**: This board uses NodeMCU firmware with Lua as the programming language. Official website: `http://www.nodemcu.com/`.

- **SparkFun ESP8266 Thing**: This is developed by SparkFun. You should use serial hardware, for instance, FTDI, to write programs to this board, but this product is ready for a LiPo charger. You can read more about it at `https://www.sparkfun.com/products/13231`.

- **SparkFun ESP8266 Thing-Dev**: This board already includes a FTDI-to-USB tool, but no LiPo charger. It's developed by SparkFun, and product information can be read at `https://www.sparkfun.com/products/13711`.

- **SparkFun Blynk board – ESP8266**: This board includes temperature and humidity sensor devices. You can read about it at `https://www.sparkfun.com/products/13794`.

- **Adafruit HUZZAH with ESP8266 Wi-Fi**: This is developed by Adafruit. Product information can be found at `https://www.adafruit.com/products/2821`.

If you're interested in the ESP8266 chip, I recommend you join the ESP8266 forum at `http://www.esp8266.com`. The following is a list of product forms for NodeMCU v2 and SparkFun ESP8266 Thing.

The following figure shows a NodeMCU v2 board:

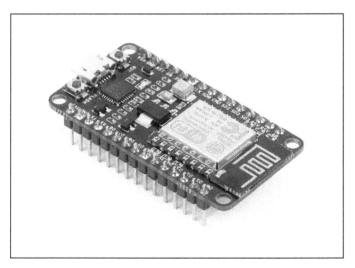

Source: `http://www.seeedstudio.com/depot/NodeMCU-v2-Lua-based-ESP8266-development-kit-p-2415.html`

Although NodeMCU v2 and SparkFun ESP8266 Thing boards have the same chip, their chip model is different. NodeMCU v2 uses an ESP8266 module. The SparkFun ESP8266 Thing board uses an ESP8266EX chip. In addition, the SparkFun ESP8266 Thing board provides a LiPo connector, which you can attach to an external battery.

The following figure shows a SparkFun ESP8266 Thing board:

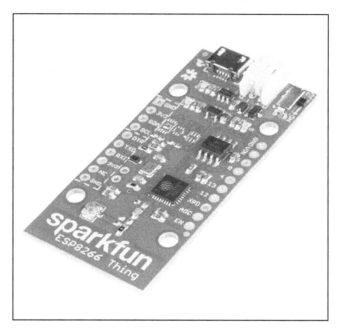

SparkFun ESP8266 Thing board. Source: `https://www.sparkfun.com/products/13231`

IoT boards-based TI CC3200 MCU

TI CC3200 is a Wi-Fi MCU based on the ARM® Cortex®-M4 from Texas Instruments. This board is a complete solution for IoT. This chip supports for station, access point, and Wi-Fi direct modes. In terms of security, TI CC3200 supports WPA2 personal and enterprise security and WPS 2.0. You can review this module at `http://www.ti.com/product/cc3200`.

For IoT development, Texas Instruments provides the SimpleLink Wi-Fi CC3200 LaunchPad evaluation kit, which is a complete kit for development and debugging.

The following figure shows a SimpleLink Wi-Fi CC3200 LaunchPad board:

Source: https://www.conrad.de/de/entwicklungsboard-texas-instruments-cc3200-launchxl-1273804.html

The TI CC3200 is also used by Readbear, http://redbear.cc, to develop RedBearLab CC3200 and RedBearLab Wi-Fi Micro boards. These boards have the same functionalities as the SimpleLink Wi-Fi CC3200 LaunchPad board, but it excludes the CC3200 debugger tool. These boards' prices are also lower than that of the SimpleLink Wi-Fi CC3200 LaunchPad board.

The following figure shows a RedBearLab CC3200 board:

Source: http://www.exp-tech.de/redbearlab-cc3200

Sensing and actuating on IoT devices

In this section, we will learn how to sense and actuate on IoT devices. This part is important because we can gather data through sensor devices or interact with the environment through actuator devices. For testing, I use Arduino, from `Arduino.cc`, and Raspberry Pi boards.

Sensing and actuating on Arduino devices

Most Arduino development uses Sketch. This is a simple programming language for building Arduino applications. If you have experience in C/C++, you'll be familiar with the programming syntax.

To start your development, you can download Arduino software from `https://www.arduino.cc/en/Main/Software`. After that, read about Arduino API at `http://www.arduino.cc/en/Reference/HomePage`.

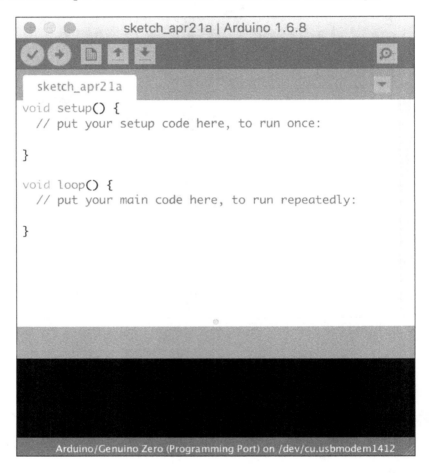

Related to digital and analog I/O, you should be familiar with the following Sketch API:

- `digitalRead()` reads data from a digital pin on Arduino
- `digitalWrite()` writes data to a digital pin on Arduino
- `analogRead()` reads analog data from an analog pin on Arduino
- `analogWrite()` writes analog data to an analog pin on Arduino

In this section, I'll show you how to work with analog and digital I/O on Arduino. I use a light sensor. LDR or Photoresistor sensors are low-priced light sensor device. Even Seeedstudio has already designed one in module form, Grove – Light Sensor(P). You can review it at `http://www.seeedstudio.com/depot/Grove-Light-SensorP-p-1253.html`. This module has four pins, but you only connect the VCC and GND pins to the VCC and GND pins of your Arduino board. Then, the SIG pin is connected to an analog pin of the Arduino board. The following figure shows a Grove – **Light Sensor(P)**:

Source: `http://www.seeedstudio.com/depot/Grove-Light-SensorP-p-1253.html`

You will need the following resources for testing:

- Jumper cables
- Light sensor module, `http://www.seeedstudio.com/depot/Grove-Light-SensorP-p-1253.html`

Now you can connect digital 6 to digital 7. Then, the SIG pin from the LDR module is connected to A0. The VCC and GND pins of the LDR module are connected to 3V3 and GND. You can see the hardware wiring in the following figure:

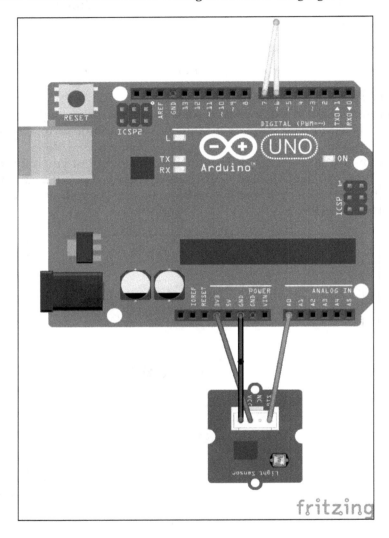

This wiring is built using Fritzing, http://fritzing.org. It's available for Windows, Linux, and Mac. You can build your own wiring with some electronics components and boards. This tool provides a lot of electronics components. You can also add your own electronics components or downloads from the Internet.

My wiring implementation is shown in the following figure:

The next step is to write an Arduino program. Open your Arduino software, then, write the following program:

```
int dig_output = 7;
int dig_input = 6;
int analog_input = A0;

int digital_val = LOW;

void setup() {
  Serial.begin(9600);

  pinMode(dig_output, OUTPUT);
  pinMode(dig_input, INPUT);
}
```

```
void loop() {

  digitalWrite(dig_output,digital_val);
  int read_digital = digitalRead(dig_input);
  Serial.print("Digital write: ");
  Serial.print(digital_val);
  Serial.print(" read: ");
  Serial.println(read_digital);

  int ldr = analogRead(analog_input);
  Serial.print("Analog read: ");
  Serial.println(ldr);

  if(digital_val==LOW)
    digital_val = HIGH;
  else
    digital_val = LOW;

  delay(1000);
}
```

Save this program as `ArduinoIO`. You can deploy this program to your Arduino board through Arduino software.

When finished, you can open the Serial Monitor tool from your Arduino software:

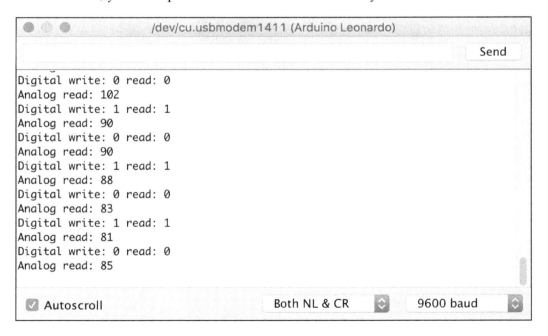

This program sends digital data (high and low values) from digital pin 7 to digital pin 6. You can read a light value from the LDR module via `analogRead()` on the A0 pin.

For the second sensing testing scenario, we will try to read temperature and humidity data from a sensor device. I use DHT-22. The RHT03 (also known as DHT-22) is a low-cost humidity and temperature sensor with a single wire digital interface. You can obtain this module from SparkFun, `https://www.sparkfun.com/products/10167`, and Adafruit, `https://www.adafruit.com/products/393`. You could also find this module in your local electronics store or online.

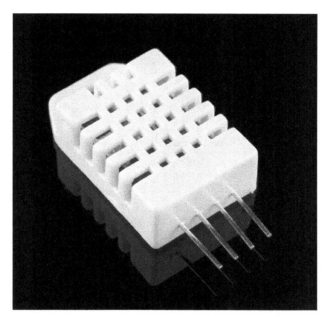

DHT22 module. `Source: https://www.adafruit.com/products/385`

Further information about the DHT-22 module, you can read the DHT-22 datasheet at `http://cdn.sparkfun.com/datasheets/Sensors/Weather/RHT03.pdf`.

Now we connect DHT-22 module to Arduino. The following is the wiring:

- VDD (pin 1) is connected to the V3V pin on Arduino
- SIG (pin 2) is connected to digital pin 8 on Arduino
- GND (pin 4) is connected to GND on Arduino

You can see this wiring in the following figure:

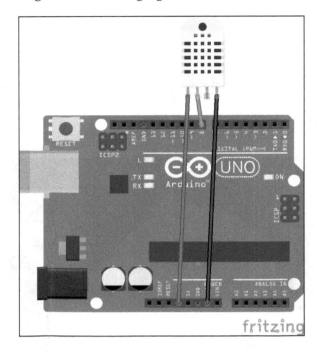

You can see my wiring implementation in the following figure:

To access DHT-22 on Arduino, we can use the DHT Sensor library from Adafruit, `https://github.com/adafruit/DHT-sensor-library`. We can install this library from the Arduino software. Click the menu **Sketch | Include Library | Manage Libraries** so you will get a dialog.

Search `dht` in **Library Manager**. You should see the DHT sensor library by Adafruit. Install this library:

When installation is complete, you can start to write programs on the Arduino software. The following is a program sample for reading temperature and humidity from the DHT-22 module:

```
#include "DHT.h"

// define DHT22
#define DHTTYPE DHT22
// define pin on DHT22
#define DHTPIN 8
```

```
DHT dht(DHTPIN, DHTTYPE);

void setup() {
  Serial.begin(9600);
  dht.begin();
}

void loop() {
  delay(2000);

  // Reading temperature or humidity takes about 250 milliseconds!
  // Sensor readings may also be up to 2 seconds 'old' (its a very
slow sensor)
  float h = dht.readHumidity();
  // Read temperature as Celsius (the default)
  float t = dht.readTemperature();


  // Check if any reads failed and exit early (to try again).
  if (isnan(h) || isnan(t)) {
    Serial.println("Failed to read from DHT sensor!");
    return;
  }

  // Compute heat index in Celsius (isFahreheit = false)
  float hic = dht.computeHeatIndex(t, h, false);

  Serial.print("Humidity: ");
  Serial.print(h);
  Serial.print(" %\t");
  Serial.print("Temperature: ");
  Serial.print(t);
  Serial.print(" *C\t");
  Serial.print("Heat index: ");
  Serial.print(hic);
  Serial.println(" *C ");
}
```

Save this program as ArduinoDHT. Now you can compile and upload the program to your Arduino board. After that, open Serial Monitor to see the temperature and humidity data:

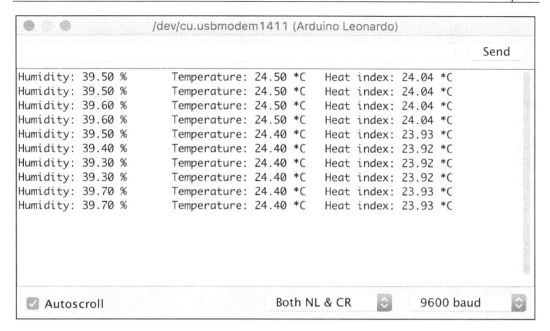

How does it work?

In the setup() function, we initialize the DHT module by calling dht.begin(). To read temperature and humidity, you can use dht.readTemperature() and dht.readHumidity(). You also can get a heat index using the dht. computeHeatIndex() function.

Sensing and actuating on Raspberry Pi devices

Raspberry Pi board is one of boards used for testing experiments in this book. In this section, we use Raspberry Pi to sense and actuate with external devices. I use a Raspberry Pi 3 board for testing.

Setting up

Before you use a Raspberry Pi board, you need to set up an OS on the board. OS software can be deployed on a microSD card. It's recommended to use an 8-GB microSD card . There's a lot of OS software you can use on a Raspberry Pi board. You can check it out at https://www.raspberrypi.org/downloads/.

For testing purposes, I use Raspbian, `https://www.raspberrypi.org/downloads/raspbian/`, as the OS on my Raspberry Pi board. Raspbian is an operating system, based on Debian, optimized for Raspberry Pi. Follow the installation guidelines at `https://www.raspberrypi.org/documentation/installation/installing-images/README.md`. Raspbian is just one OS for Raspberry Pi OS. You can try other Raspberry Pi OSes at `https://www.raspberrypi.org/downloads/`.

Accessing Raspberry Pi GPIO

If you use the latest version of Raspbian (Jessie or later), wiringPi module, `http://wiringpi.com`, is already installed for you. You can verify your wiringPi version on Raspberry Pi Terminal using the following command:

```
$ gpio -v
```

You should see your wiringPi module version. A sample of the program output can be seen in the following screenshot:

```
Documents — pi@raspberrypi: ~ — ssh pi@192.168.0.12 — 80×17

[pi@raspberrypi:~ $ gpio -v
gpio version: 2.32
Copyright (c) 2012-2015 Gordon Henderson
This is free software with ABSOLUTELY NO WARRANTY.
For details type: gpio -warranty

Raspberry Pi Details:
  Type: Pi 3, Revision: 02, Memory: 1024MB, Maker: Sony
  * Device tree is enabled.
  * This Raspberry Pi supports user-level GPIO access.
    -> See the man-page for more details
    -> ie. export WIRINGPI_GPIOMEM=1
pi@raspberrypi:~ $
```

Furthermore, you can verify the Raspberry GPIO layout using the following command:

```
$ gpio - readall
```

This command will display the Raspberry Pi layout. It can detect your Raspberry Pi model. A sample of the program output for my board, Raspberry Pi 3, can be seen in the following screenshot:

```
 ● ● ●          Documents — pi@raspberrypi: ~ — ssh pi@192.168.0.12 — 80×28
[pi@raspberrypi:~ $ gpio readall
 +-----+-----+---------+------+---+---Pi 3---+---+------+---------+-----+-----+
 | BCM | wPi |   Name  | Mode | V | Physical | V | Mode |   Name  | wPi | BCM |
 +-----+-----+---------+------+---+----++----+---+------+---------+-----+-----+
 |     |     |    3.3v |      |   |  1 || 2  |   |      | 5v      |     |     |
 |   2 |   8 |   SDA.1 |   IN | 1 |  3 || 4  |   |      | 5V      |     |     |
 |   3 |   9 |   SCL.1 |   IN | 1 |  5 || 6  |   |      | 0v      |     |     |
 |   4 |   7 | GPIO. 7 |   IN | 1 |  7 || 8  | 1 | ALT5 | TxD     |  15 |  14 |
 |     |     |      0v |      |   |  9 || 10 | 1 | ALT5 | RxD     |  16 |  15 |
 |  17 |   0 | GPIO. 0 |   IN | 0 | 11 || 12 | 0 | IN   | GPIO. 1 |  1  |  18 |
 |  27 |   2 | GPIO. 2 |   IN | 0 | 13 || 14 |   |      | 0v      |     |     |
 |  22 |   3 | GPIO. 3 |   IN | 0 | 15 || 16 | 0 | IN   | GPIO. 4 |  4  |  23 |
 |     |     |    3.3v |      |   | 17 || 18 | 0 | IN   | GPIO. 5 |  5  |  24 |
 |  10 |  12 |    MOSI |   IN | 0 | 19 || 20 |   |      | 0v      |     |     |
 |   9 |  13 |    MISO |   IN | 0 | 21 || 22 | 0 | IN   | GPIO. 6 |  6  |  25 |
 |  11 |  14 |    SCLK |   IN | 0 | 23 || 24 | 1 | IN   | CE0     |  10 |  8  |
 |     |     |      0v |      |   | 25 || 26 | 1 | IN   | CE1     |  11 |  7  |
 |   0 |  30 |   SDA.0 |   IN | 1 | 27 || 28 | 1 | IN   | SCL.0   |  31 |  1  |
 |   5 |  21 | GPIO.21 |   IN | 1 | 29 || 30 |   |      | 0v      |     |     |
 |   6 |  22 | GPIO.22 |   IN | 1 | 31 || 32 | 0 | IN   | GPIO.26 |  26 |  12 |
 |  13 |  23 | GPIO.23 |   IN | 0 | 33 || 34 |   |      | 0v      |     |     |
 |  19 |  24 | GPIO.24 |   IN | 0 | 35 || 36 | 0 | IN   | GPIO.27 |  27 |  16 |
 |  26 |  25 | GPIO.25 |   IN | 0 | 37 || 38 | 0 | IN   | GPIO.28 |  28 |  20 |
 |     |     |      0v |      |   | 39 || 40 | 0 | IN   | GPIO.29 |  29 |  21 |
 +-----+-----+---------+------+---+----++----+---+------+---------+-----+-----+
 | BCM | wPi |   Name  | Mode | V | Physical | V | Mode |   Name  | wPi | BCM |
 +-----+-----+---------+------+---+---Pi 3---+---+------+---------+-----+-----+
pi@raspberrypi:~ $ █
```

For Raspberry Pi GPIO development, the latest Raspbian also has the RPi.GPIO library already installed—https://pypi.python.org/pypi/RPi.GPIO, for Python, so we can use it directly now.

To test Raspberry Pi GPIO, we put an LED on GPIO11 (BCM 17). You can see the wiring in the following figure:

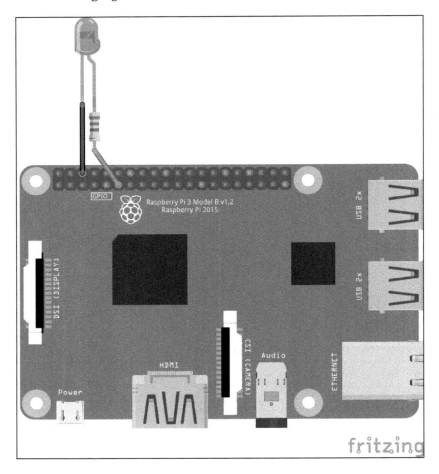

Now you can write a Python program with your own editor. Write the following program:

```
import RPi.GPIO as GPIO
import time


led_pin = 17
GPIO.setmode(GPIO.BCM)
GPIO.setup(led_pin, GPIO.OUT)
```

```
try:
    while 1:
        print("turn on led")
        GPIO.output(led_pin, GPIO.HIGH)
        time.sleep(2)
        print("turn off led")
        GPIO.output(led_pin, GPIO.LOW)
        time.sleep(2)

except KeyboardInterrupt:
    GPIO.output(led_pin, GPIO.LOW)
    GPIO.cleanup()


print("done")
```

The following is an explanation of the code:

- We set GPIO type using `GPIO.setmode(GPIO.BCM)`. I used the `GPIO.BCM` mode. In GPIO BCM, you should see GPIO values on the **BCM** column from the GPIO layout.

- We defined GPIO, which will be used by calling `GPIO.setup()` as the output mode.

- To set digital output, we can call `GPIO.output()`. `GPIO.HIGH` is used to send 1 to the digital output. Otherwise, `GPIO.LOW` is used for sending 0 to the digital output.

Save this program into a file called `ch01_led.py`.

Now you can run the program by typing the following command on your Raspberry Pi Terminal.

```
$ sudo python ch01_led.py
```

We execute the program using `sudo`, due to security permissions. To access the Raspberry Pi hardware I/O, we need local administrator privileges.

You should see a blinking LED and also get a response from the program. A sample of the program output can be seen in the following screenshot:

```
● ● ●          Documents — pi@raspberrypi: ~/Documents/book — ssh pi@192.168.0.12 — 8...
[pi@raspberrypi:~ $ cd Documents/book/
[pi@raspberrypi:~/Documents/book $ python ch01_led.py
turn on led
turn off led
turn on led
turn off led
turn on led
turn off led
turn on led
turn off led
turn on led
turn off led
turn on led
```

Sensing through sensor devices

In this section, we will explore how to sense from Raspberry Pi. We use DHT-22 to collect temperature and humidity readings on its environment.

To access DHT-22 using Python, we use the Adafruit Python DHT Sensor library. You can review this module at https://github.com/adafruit/Adafruit_Python_DHT.

You need required libraries to build Adafruit Python DHT Sensor library. Type the following commands in your Raspberry Pi Terminal:

```
$ sudo apt-get update
$ sudo apt-get install build-essential python-dev
```

Now you can download and install the Adafruit Python DHT Sensor library:

```
$ git clone https://github.com/adafruit/Adafruit_Python_DHT
$ cd Adafruit_Python_DHT/
$ sudo python setup.py install
```

If finished, we can start to build our wiring. Connect the DHT-22 module to the following connections:

- DHT-22 pin 1 (VDD) is connected to the 3.3V pin on your Raspberry Pi
- DHT-22 pin 2 (SIG) is connected to the GPIO23 (see the **BCM** column) pin on your Raspberry Pi
- DHT-22 pin 4 (GND) is connected to the GND pin on your Raspberry Pi

The complete wiring is shown in the following figure:

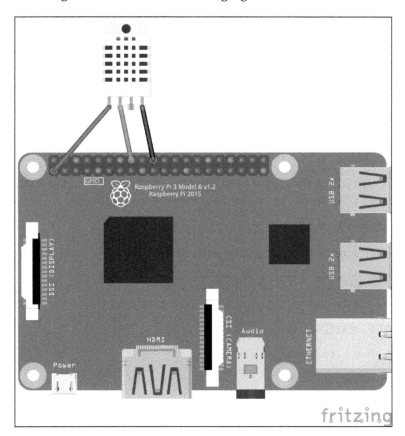

The next step is to write a Python program. You can write the following code:

```
import Adafruit_DHT
import time

sensor = Adafruit_DHT.DHT22
```

```
# DHT22 pin on Raspberry Pi
pin = 23


try:
    while 1:
        print("reading DHT22...")
        humidity, temperature = Adafruit_DHT.read_retry(sensor, pin)

        if humidity is not None and temperature is not None:
            print('Temp={0:0.1f}*C  Humidity={1:0.1f}%'.
format(temperature, humidity))

        time.sleep(2)

except KeyboardInterrupt:
    print("exit")


print("done")
```

Save this program into a file called ch01_dht22.py. Then, you can run this file on your Raspberry Pi Terminal. Type the following command:

```
$ sudo python ch01_dht22.py
```

A sample of the program output can be seen in the following screenshot:

```
Documents — pi@raspberrypi: ~/Documents/book — ssh pi@192.168.0.12 — 8...
pi@raspberrypi:~/Documents/book $ sudo python ch01_dht22.py
reading DHT22...
Temp=30.2*C  Humidity=77.6%
reading DHT22...
Temp=30.2*C  Humidity=76.0%
reading DHT22...
Temp=30.1*C  Humidity=76.0%
reading DHT22...
Temp=30.1*C  Humidity=76.0%
reading DHT22...
Temp=30.2*C  Humidity=76.1%
reading DHT22...
^Cexit
done
pi@raspberrypi:~/Documents/book $
```

How does it work?

First, we set our DHT module type by calling the `Adafruit_DHT.DHT22` object. Set which DHT-22 pin is attached to your Raspberry Pi board. In this case, I use GPIO23 (BCM).

To obtain temperature and humidity sensor data, we call `Adafruit_DHT.read_retry(sensor, pin)`. To make sure the returning values are not `NULL`, we validate them using conditional-if.

Building a smart temperature controller for your room

To control your room's temperature, we can build a smart temperature controller. In this case, we use a **PID (proportional–integral–derivative)** controller. When you set a certain temperature, a PID controller will change the temperature by turning either cooler or hotter. A PID controller program is developed using Python, which runs on the Raspberry Pi board.

Assume cooler and heater machines are connected via a relay. We can activate cooler and heater machine by sending `HIGH` signal on a relay.

Let's build!

Introducing PID controller

PID control is the most common control algorithm widely used in industry, and has been universally accepted in industrial control. The basic idea behind a PID controller is to read a sensor, then compute the desired actuator output by calculating proportional, integral, and derivative responses and summing those three components to compute the output.

An example design of a general PID controller is depicted in the following figure:

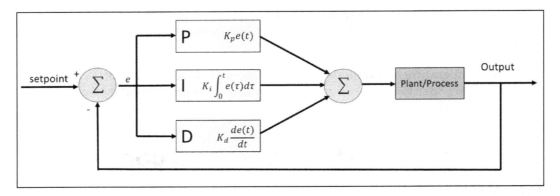

Furthermore, a PID controller formula can be defined as follows:

$$u(t) = K_p e(t) + K_i \int_0^t e(\tau)d\tau + K_d \frac{de(t)}{dt}$$

K_p, K_i, K_d represent the coefficients for the proportional, integral, and derivative. These parameters are non-negative values. The variable e represents the tracking error, the difference between the desired input value i, and the actual output y. This error signal e will be sent to the PID controller.

Implementing PID controller in Python

In this section, we will build a Python application to implement the PID controller. In general, our program flowchart can be described by the following figure:

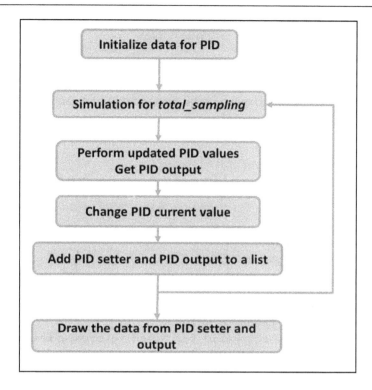

We should not build a PID library from scratch. You can translate PID controller formula into Python code easily. For implementation, I use the PID class from https://github.com/ivmech/ivPID. The following is the content of the PID.py file:

```python
import time

class PID:
    """PID Controller
    """

    def __init__(self, P=0.2, I=0.0, D=0.0):

        self.Kp = P
        self.Ki = I
        self.Kd = D

        self.sample_time = 0.00
        self.current_time = time.time()
```

```
            self.last_time = self.current_time

            self.clear()

    def clear(self):
        """Clears PID computations and coefficients"""
        self.SetPoint = 0.0

        self.PTerm = 0.0
        self.ITerm = 0.0
        self.DTerm = 0.0
        self.last_error = 0.0

        # Windup Guard
        self.int_error = 0.0
        self.windup_guard = 20.0

        self.output = 0.0

    def update(self, feedback_value):
        """Calculates PID value for given reference feedback

        .. math::
            u(t) = K_p e(t) + K_i \int_{0}^{t} e(t)dt + K_d {de}/{dt}

        .. figure::  images/pid_1.png
           :align:   center

           Test PID with Kp=1.2, Ki=1, Kd=0.001 (test_pid.py)

        """
        error = self.SetPoint - feedback_value

        self.current_time = time.time()
        delta_time = self.current_time - self.last_time
        delta_error = error - self.last_error

        if (delta_time >= self.sample_time):
            self.PTerm = self.Kp * error
            self.ITerm += error * delta_time

            if (self.ITerm < -self.windup_guard):
                self.ITerm = -self.windup_guard
            elif (self.ITerm > self.windup_guard):
```

```
                self.ITerm = self.windup_guard

            self.DTerm = 0.0
            if delta_time > 0:
                self.DTerm = delta_error / delta_time

            # Remember last time and last error for next calculation
            self.last_time = self.current_time
            self.last_error = error

            self.output = self.PTerm + (self.Ki * self.ITerm) + (self.
Kd * self.DTerm)

    def setKp(self, proportional_gain):
        """Determines how aggressively the PID reacts to the current
error with setting Proportional Gain"""
        self.Kp = proportional_gain

    def setKi(self, integral_gain):
        """Determines how aggressively the PID reacts to the current
error with setting Integral Gain"""
        self.Ki = integral_gain

    def setKd(self, derivative_gain):
        """Determines how aggressively the PID reacts to the current
error with setting Derivative Gain"""
        self.Kd = derivative_gain

    def setWindup(self, windup):
        """Integral windup, also known as integrator windup or reset
windup,
        refers to the situation in a PID feedback controller where
        a large change in setpoint occurs (say a positive change)
        and the integral terms accumulates a significant error
        during the rise (windup), thus overshooting and continuing
        to increase as this accumulated error is unwound
        (offset by errors in the other direction).
        The specific problem is the excess overshooting.
        """
        self.windup_guard = windup

    def setSampleTime(self, sample_time):
        """PID that should be updated at a regular interval.
        Based on a pre-determined sampe time, the PID decides if it
should compute or return immediately.
        """
        self.sample_time = sample_time
```

For testing purposes, we create a simple program for simulation. We need required libraries such as numpy, scipy, pandas, patsy, and matplotlib libraries. First, you should install python-dev for Python development. Type the following commands in your Raspberry Pi Terminal:

```
$ sudo apt-get update
$ sudo apt-get install python-dev
```

When done, you can install numpy, scipy, pandas, and patsy libraries. Open your Raspberry Pi Terminal and type the following commands:

```
$ sudo apt-get install python-scipy
$ pip install numpy scipy pandas patsy
```

The last step is to install the matplotlib library from source code. Type the following commands on your Raspberry Pi Terminal:

```
$ git clone https://github.com/matplotlib/matplotlib
$ cd matplotlib
$ python setup.py build
$ sudo python setup.py install
```

Once the required libraries are installed, we can test our PID.py file. Type the following program:

```python
import matplotlib
matplotlib.use('Agg')

import PID
import time
import matplotlib.pyplot as plt
import numpy as np
from scipy.interpolate import spline


P = 1.4
I = 1
D = 0.001
pid = PID.PID(P, I, D)

pid.SetPoint = 0.0
pid.setSampleTime(0.01)
```

```
total_sampling = 100
feedback = 0

feedback_list = []
time_list = []
setpoint_list = []

print("simulating....")
for i in range(1, total_sampling):
    pid.update(feedback)
    output = pid.output
    if pid.SetPoint > 0:
        feedback += (output - (1 / i))

    if 20 < i < 60:
        pid.SetPoint = 1

    if 60 <= i < 80:
        pid.SetPoint = 0.5

    if i >= 80:
        pid.SetPoint = 1.3

    time.sleep(0.02)

    feedback_list.append(feedback)
    setpoint_list.append(pid.SetPoint)
    time_list.append(i)

time_sm = np.array(time_list)
time_smooth = np.linspace(time_sm.min(), time_sm.max(), 300)
feedback_smooth = spline(time_list, feedback_list, time_smooth)

fig1 = plt.gcf()
fig1.subplots_adjust(bottom=0.15)

plt.plot(time_smooth, feedback_smooth, color='red')
plt.plot(time_list, setpoint_list, color='blue')
plt.xlim((0, total_sampling))
plt.ylim((min(feedback_list) - 0.5, max(feedback_list) + 0.5))
plt.xlabel('time (s)')
plt.ylabel('PID (PV)')
```

```
plt.title('TEST PID')


plt.grid(True)
print("saving...")
fig1.savefig('result.png', dpi=100)
```

Save this program into a file called `test_pid.py`. Then, run this program.

$ python test_pid.py

This program will generate `result.png` as a result of the PID process. A sample of the output form, `result.png`, is shown in the following figure. You can see that the blue line represents desired values and the red line is an output of PID:

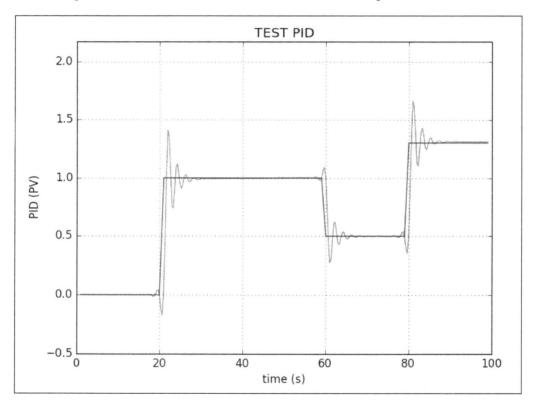

How does it work?

First, we define our PID parameters, as follows:

```
P = 1.4
I = 1
D = 0.001
pid = PID.PID(P, I, D)

pid.SetPoint = 0.0
pid.setSampleTime(0.01)

total_sampling = 100
feedback = 0

feedback_list = []
time_list = []
setpoint_list = []
```

After that, we compute the PID value during sampling time. In this case, we set the desired output value as follows:

- Desired output 1 for sampling from 20 to 60
- Desired output 0.5 for sampling from 60 to 80
- Desired output 1.3 for sampling more than 80

```
for i in range(1, total_sampling):
    pid.update(feedback)
    output = pid.output
    if pid.SetPoint > 0:
        feedback += (output - (1 / i))

    if 20 < i < 60:
        pid.SetPoint = 1

    if 60 <= i < 80:
        pid.SetPoint = 0.5

    if i >= 80:
        pid.SetPoint = 1.3

    time.sleep(0.02)

    feedback_list.append(feedback)
    setpoint_list.append(pid.SetPoint)
time_list.append(i)
```

The last step is to generate a report and is saved to a file called `result.png`:

```
time_sm = np.array(time_list)
time_smooth = np.linspace(time_sm.min(), time_sm.max(), 300)
feedback_smooth = spline(time_list, feedback_list, time_smooth)

fig1 = plt.gcf()
fig1.subplots_adjust(bottom=0.15)

plt.plot(time_smooth, feedback_smooth, color='red')
plt.plot(time_list, setpoint_list, color='blue')
plt.xlim((0, total_sampling))
plt.ylim((min(feedback_list) - 0.5, max(feedback_list) + 0.5))
plt.xlabel('time (s)')
plt.ylabel('PID (PV)')
plt.title('TEST PID')


plt.grid(True)
print("saving...")
fig1.savefig('result.png', dpi=100)
```

Controlling room temperature using PID controller

Now we can change our PID controller simulation using the real application. We use DHT-22 to check a room temperature. The output of measurement is used as feedback input for the PID controller.

If the PID output positive value, then we turn on heater. Otherwise, we activate cooler machine. It may not good approach but this good point to show how PID controller work.

We attach DHT-22 to GPIO23 (BCM). Let's write the following program:

```
import matplotlib
matplotlib.use('Agg')

import PID
import Adafruit_DHT
import time
import matplotlib.pyplot as plt
import numpy as np
```

```python
from scipy.interpolate import spline

sensor = Adafruit_DHT.DHT22

# DHT22 pin on Raspberry Pi
pin = 23

P = 1.4
I = 1
D = 0.001
pid = PID.PID(P, I, D)

pid.SetPoint = 0.0
pid.setSampleTime(0.25)  # a second

total_sampling = 100
sampling_i = 0
measurement = 0
feedback = 0

feedback_list = []
time_list = []
setpoint_list = []

print('PID controller is running..')
try:
    while 1:
        pid.update(feedback)
        output = pid.output

        humidity, temperature = Adafruit_DHT.read_retry(sensor, pin)
        if humidity is not None and temperature is not None:
            if pid.SetPoint > 0:
                feedback += temperature + output

            print('i={0} desired.temp={1:0.1f}*C temp={2:0.1f}*C pid.
out={3:0.1f} feedback={4:0.1f}'
                    .format(sampling_i, pid.SetPoint, temperature,
output, feedback))
            if output > 0:
                print('turn on heater')
            elif output < 0:
                print('turn on cooler')
```

```
            if 20 < sampling_i < 60:
                pid.SetPoint = 28  # celsius

            if 60 <= sampling_i < 80:
                pid.SetPoint = 25  # celsius

            if sampling_i >= 80:
                pid.SetPoint = 20  # celsius

            time.sleep(0.5)
            sampling_i += 1

            feedback_list.append(feedback)
            setpoint_list.append(pid.SetPoint)
            time_list.append(sampling_i)

            if sampling_i >= total_sampling:
                break

except KeyboardInterrupt:
    print("exit")


print("pid controller done.")
print("generating a report...")
time_sm = np.array(time_list)
time_smooth = np.linspace(time_sm.min(), time_sm.max(), 300)
feedback_smooth = spline(time_list, feedback_list, time_smooth)

fig1 = plt.gcf()
fig1.subplots_adjust(bottom=0.15, left=0.1)

plt.plot(time_smooth, feedback_smooth, color='red')
plt.plot(time_list, setpoint_list, color='blue')
plt.xlim((0, total_sampling))
plt.ylim((min(feedback_list) - 0.5, max(feedback_list) + 0.5))
plt.xlabel('time (s)')
```

```
plt.ylabel('PID (PV)')
plt.title('Temperature PID Controller')


plt.grid(True)
fig1.savefig('pid_temperature.png', dpi=100)
print("finish")
```

Save this program to a file called ch01_pid.py. Now you can this program:

$ sudo python ch01_pid.py

After executing the program, you should obtain a file called pid_temperature.png. A sample output of this file can be seen in the following figure:

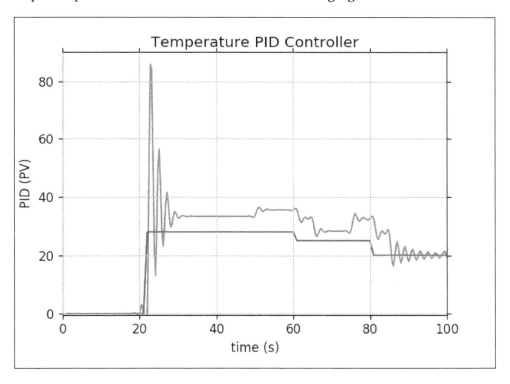

If I don't take any action either turning on a cooler or turning on a heater, I obtain a result, shown in the following figure:

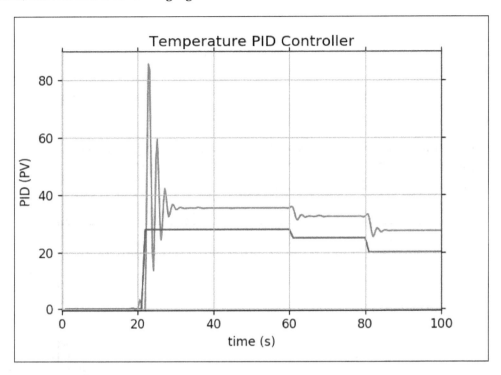

How does it work?

Generally speaking, this program combines our two topics: reading current temperature through DHT-22 and implementing a PID controller. After measuring the temperature, we send this value to the PID controller program. The output of PID will take a certain action. In this case, it will turn on cooler and heater machines.

Summary

In this chapter, we have reviewed some basic statistics and explored various Python libraries related to statistics and data science. We also learned about several IoT device platforms and how to sense and actuate.

For the last topic, we deployed a PID controller as a study sample how to integrate a controller system on an IoT project. In the following chapter, we will learn how to build a decision system for our IoT project.

References

The following is a list of recommended books from which you can learn more about the topics in this chapter:

1. Richard D. De Veaux, Paul F. Velleman, and David E. Bock, *Stats Data and Models*, 4th Edition, 2015, *Pearson Publishing*.

2. Sheldon M. Ross, *Introductory Statistics*, 3rd Edition, Academic Press, 2010.

2
Decision System for IoT Projects

If we feel a cold, then we use a jacket. When we are hungry, we decide to eat. These decisions can be made by us, but how does a machine make a decision? In this chapter, we learn how to build a decision system which can be implemented on IoT devices.

We explore the following topics:

- Introduction to decision system and machine learning
- Exploring Python libraries to build a decision system
- Building a simple decision system-based Bayesian theory
- Integrating a decision system and IoT project
- Building your own decision system-based IoT

Introduction to decision system and machine learning

A decision system is a system that makes a decision based on several input parameters. A decision system is built on decision theories. Being human involves making decisions for almost life cases.

The following are examples of decisions that humans take:

- Shall I buy the car today? The decision depends on my preferences. This car looks fine, but it is too expensive for me.

- Shall I bring an umbrella today? This decision depends on the current condition in the area where we are staying. If it is cloudy, it's better to bring an umbrella even though it may not rain.

Generally speaking, we teach a machine such as a computer in order to understand and achieve a specific goal. This case is called machine learning. Varieties of programs are implemented in machines so they can make decisions.

Machine learning consists of various algorithms to build a decision system. In this book, I use fuzzy logic and Bayesian algorithms to make a decision system. I explain them in the next section.

Decision system-based Bayesian

Bayesian uses the manipulation of conditional probabilities approach to interpret data. In this section, we build a decision system using the Bayesian method.

Consider D, called the decision space, which denotes the space of all possible decisions d that could be chosen by the **decision maker (DM).** Θ is the space of all possible outcomes or state of nature ω, $\omega \in \Theta$.

Decision system-based Bayesian is built by Bayesian theory. For illustration, I show a simple spam filter using Bayesian. Imagine the sample space X is the set of all possible datasets of words, from which a single dataset word x will result. For each $\omega \in \Theta$ and $x \in X$, the sampling model $P(\omega)$ describes a belief that x would be the outcome of spam probability. $P(x|\omega)$, prior distribution, is the true population characteristics and supposes a spam probability for x.$P(\omega|x)$., posterior distribution, describes a belief that ω is the true value of spam, having observed dataset x.

The posterior distribution is obtained using Bayes' rule as follows:

$$P(\omega|x) = \frac{P(x|\omega)P(\omega)}{P(x)}$$

This result will return a spam probability value.

Now we can build a decision system. Consider $\lambda\ (\omega,d)$ is a lost function that states exactly how costly each action d is. Lost function $\lambda(d_i|\omega_i)$ is the loss incurred for taking action d_i, where the class is ω_i. The expected loss or conditional risk is defined as follows:

$$R(d_i|x) = \sum_{j=1}^{c} \lambda(d_i|\omega_j)P(\omega_j|x)$$

A decision function $d(x)$ is a mapping from observations to actions. The total risk of a decision function can be calculated as given in the following equation:

$$E_{P(x)}[R(d(x)|x)] = \sum_{x} P(x)R(d(x)|x)$$

A decision function is optimal if it minimizes the total risk. A decision is made based on a minimum risk value for each action.

This is a simple explanation. To get further information about Bayesian theory, I suggest you read a textbook about Bayesian.

Decision system-based fuzzy logic

Consider you want to make a decision based on the current temperature, for instance, if the room's temperature is 30°C, then you turn on a cooler machine. Otherwise, if the room's temperature is 18°C, you turn on a heater machine.

This decision happens because we already defined exact values for turning on the machines. What's happening is that we say that we want to turn on the cooler machine if the room's temperature is hot. Furthermore, we also want to turn on the heater machine if the room's temperature is cold.

Cold and hot are two terms related to human linguistics. We should determine how cold and hot criteria are. A human differentiates the criteria for cold and hot, but how can a computer and machine know?

This problem can be solved using fuzzy logic. The idea of fuzzy logic was first introduced by Dr. Lotfi Zadeh from the University of California at Berkeley in the 1960s. The theory of fuzzy logic is developed with fuzzy sets and memberships.

In general, decision system-based fuzzy logic is described in the following figure:

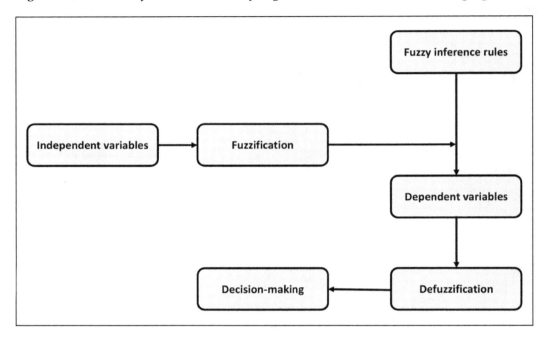

We can build a decision system with the following steps:

1. Define independent variables that represent your problem. This step is a part of the extraction process. These variables usually have numeric values.

2. Build fuzzy sets that consist of linguistic variables, for instance, cold, warm and hot.

3. Execute the fuzzification process, which transforms independent variables (numerical values) to dependent variables (linguistic values).

4. Build fuzzy inference rules to map between a given input and an output. We can use the if-then approach.

5. After aggregating all outputs, we do defuzzification to obtain a single number.

From the output of single number, we can make a decision. We do an experiment on how to build a decision system using fuzzy logic in the next section.

Python libraries for building a decision system

In this section, we explore some Python libraries to build our decision system. I focus on Bayesian and fuzzy logic models for implementing the decision system.

Bayesian

We can implement Bayesian probability using Python. For our demo, we generate output values from two independent variables, x_1 and x_2. The output model is defined as follows:

$$y = \alpha + \beta_1 x_1 + \beta_2 x_2 + c\sigma$$

c is a random value. We define α, β_1, β_2, and σ as 0.5, 1, 2.5, and 0.5.

These independent variables are generated using a random object from the NumPy library. After that, we compute the model with these variables.

We can implement this case with the following scripts:

```
import matplotlib
matplotlib.use('Agg')

import numpy as np
import matplotlib.pyplot as plt

# initialization
np.random.seed(100)
alpha, sigma = 0.5, 0.5
beta = [1, 2.5]
size = 100
```

```
# Predictor variable
X1 = np.random.randn(size)
X2 = np.random.randn(size) * 0.37

# Simulate outcome variable
Y = alpha + beta[0]*X1 + beta[1]*X2 + np.random.randn(size)*sigma

fig, ax = plt.subplots(1, 2, sharex=True, figsize=(10, 4))
fig.subplots_adjust(bottom=0.15, left=0.1)

ax[0].scatter(X1, Y)
ax[1].scatter(X2, Y)
ax[0].set_ylabel('Y')
ax[0].set_xlabel('X1')
ax[1].set_xlabel('X2')


plt.grid(True)
fig.savefig('predict.png', dpi=100)
print("finish")
```

You can save these scripts into a file, called ch02_predict.py.

Then, you can run the program by typing this command:

$ python ch02_predict.py

This program will generate a PNG file, predict.png, which is depicted as follows:

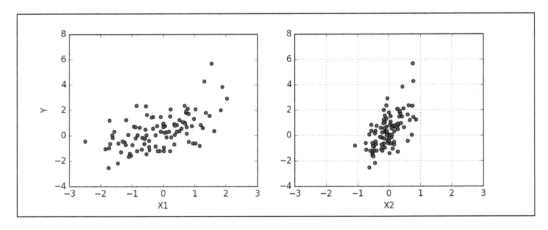

The program is simple, generating the independent variables via NumPy. Thus, we plot the model using the `matplotlib` library.

Now we try to use the Python library to build a Bayesian model. One of Python's libraries for Bayesian computing is PyMC, which provides Bayesian statistical models and fitting algorithms, including Markov Chain Monte Carlo. PyMC is an open source library. You can review and download it at `https://github.com/pymc-devs/pymc`.

To install the PyMC library, you can use `easy_install` or `pip`. If you want to install PyMC using `easy_install`, you type this command:

`$ easy_install pymc`

You may need administrator level (sudo) to perform PyMC installation via `easy_install`. Another option is to install it via `pip`.

`$ pip install pymc`

To test PyMC, we use example codes from PyMC. The first step to implement Bayesian computing is to build a model. In this scenario, we use normal distribution for prior parameters.

$$\theta(x) = \frac{e^{a+bx}}{(1 + e^{a+bx})}$$

Now we can implement this problem using PyMC. Write the following script:

```python
import pymc
import numpy as np

# Some data
n = 5 * np.ones(4, dtype=int)
x = np.array([-.86, -.3, -.05, .73])

# Priors on unknown parameters
alpha = pymc.Normal('alpha', mu=0, tau=.01)
beta = pymc.Normal('beta', mu=0, tau=.01)

# Arbitrary deterministic function of parameters
@pymc.deterministic
def theta(a=alpha, b=beta):
    """theta = logit^{-1}(a+b)"""
```

```
      return pymc.invlogit(a + b * x)
# Binomial likelihood for data
d = pymc.Binomial('d', n=n, p=theta, value=np.array([0., 1., 3., 5.]),
               observed=True)
```

Save this model into a file, called `mymodel.py`.

Our model will be used in a simulation through **Markov Chain Monte Carlo (MCMC)** method. We will obtain posterior values from that simulation.

Let's create a file, called `ch02_pymc.py` and write the following scripts:

```
import matplotlib
matplotlib.use('Agg')

import pymc
import mymodel

S = pymc.MCMC(mymodel, db='pickle')
S.sample(iter=10000, burn=5000, thin=2)

pymc.Matplot.plot(S)
print("finish")
```

You can run this program on a Raspberry Pi Terminal by typing this command:

$ python ch02_pymc.py

If the program runs well, you can see the output shown in the following screenshot:

This program will also generate three files, `alpha.png`, `beta.png`, and `theta-3.png`. A sample of `alpha.png` file is depicted in the following screenshot:

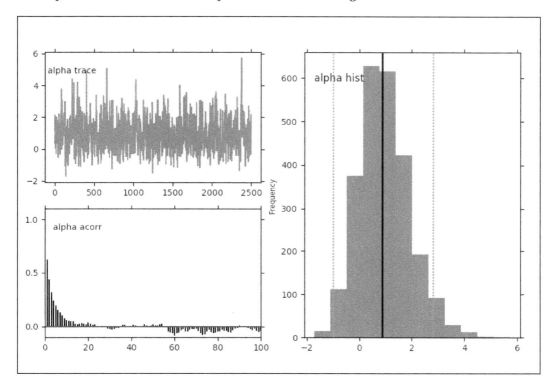

You can see alpha values, which are random values with Normal distribution `alpha.png`. Furthermore, beta values are generated with Normal distribution. You can see beta values in the `beta.png` file in the following screenshot:

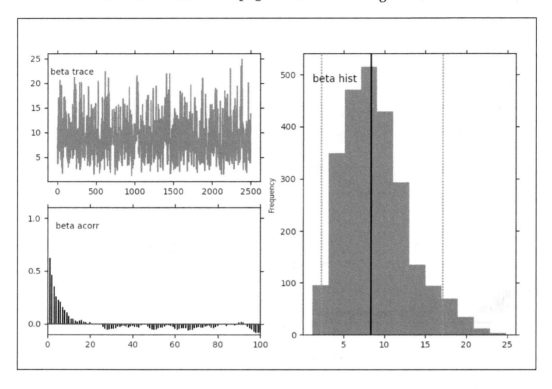

The last of the program output is the `theta-3.png` file, which shows how theta values are computed by a formula. You can see it in the following screenshot:

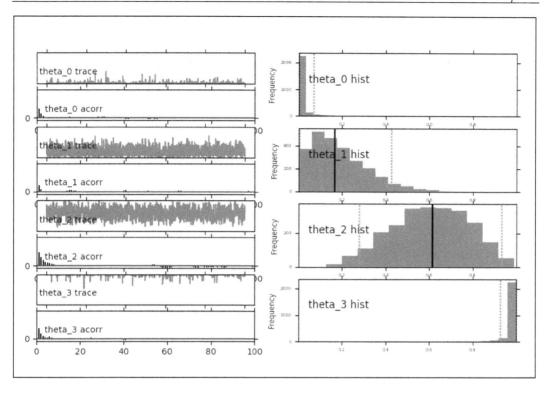

Fuzzy logic

One of the famous Python libraries for fuzzy logic is scikit-fuzzy. Several fuzzy logic algorithms have already been implemented on this library. Since scikit-fuzzy is an open source library, you can review the source code on this site, https://github.com/scikit-fuzzy/scikit-fuzzy.

Before you install this library, you should already have installed NumPy and SciPy libraries. You can install scikit-fuzzy via pip. Type this command:

```
$ sudo pip install scikit-fuzzy
```

As another option, you can install the `scikit-fuzzy` library from source code. Type these commands:

```
$ git clone https://github.com/scikit-fuzzy/scikit-fuzzy
$ cd scikit-fuzzy/
$ sudo python setup.py install
```

After completing the installation, you can use `scikit-fuzzy`.

To test how to work with `scikit-fuzzy`, we will build a fuzzy membership for temperature using the `fuzz.trimf()` function. You can write the following scripts:

```python
import matplotlib
matplotlib.use('Agg')


import numpy as np
import skfuzzy as fuzz
import matplotlib.pyplot as plt

# Generate universe variables
x_temp = np.arange(0, 11, 1)

# Generate fuzzy membership functions
temp_lo = fuzz.trimf(x_temp, [0, 0, 5])
temp_md = fuzz.trimf(x_temp, [0, 5, 10])
temp_hi = fuzz.trimf(x_temp, [5, 10, 10])

# Visualize these universes and membership functions
fig, ax = plt.subplots()

ax.plot(x_temp, temp_lo, 'b--', linewidth=1.5, label='Cold')
ax.plot(x_temp, temp_md, 'g-', linewidth=1.5, label='Warm')
ax.plot(x_temp, temp_hi, 'r:', linewidth=1.5, label='Hot')
ax.set_title('Temperature')
ax.legend()

ax.spines['top'].set_visible(False)
ax.spines['right'].set_visible(False)
ax.get_xaxis().tick_bottom()
ax.get_yaxis().tick_left()
ax.set_ylabel('Fuzzy membership')
```

```
plt.tight_layout()

print('saving...')
plt.grid(True)
fig.savefig('fuzzy_membership.png', dpi=100)
print('done')
```

Save these scripts into a file called ch02_skfuzzy.py.

Now you can run this file by typing this command:

```
$ python ch02_skfuzzy.py
```

This program will generate a fuzzy_membership.png file. A sample of this file is depicted as follows:

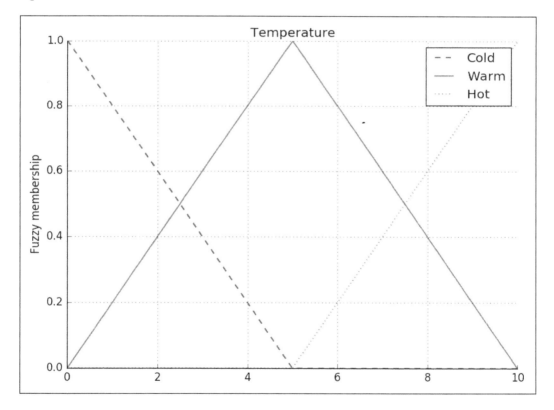

Building a simple decision system-based Bayesian theory

In this section, we build a simple decision system using Bayesian theory. A smart water system is a smart system that controls water. In general, you can see the system architecture in the following figure:

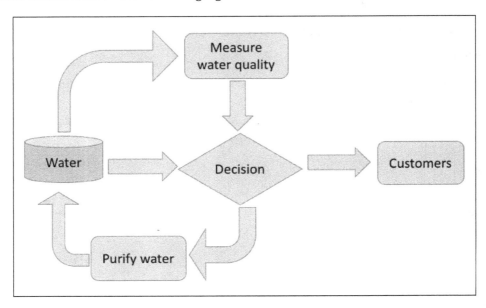

After using a sensing process on water to obtain the water quality, you can make a decision. If the water quality is good, we can transfer the water to customers. Otherwise, we purify the water.

To implement a decision system-based Bayesian theory, firstly we define the state of nature. In this case, we define two states of nature:

- ω_1: water is ready for drinking
- ω_2: water should be cleaned (kotor)

For inputs, we can declare x_1 and x_1 as negative and positive as the observation results.

We define prior values and class conditional probabilities as follows:

$$P(\omega_1) = 0.8$$
$$P(\omega_2) = 0.2$$
$$P(x_1|\omega_1) = 0.3$$
$$P(x_1|\omega_2) = 0.7$$
$$P(x_2|\omega_1) = 0.2$$
$$P(x_2|\omega_2) = 0.8$$

To build a decision, we should make a loss function The following is a loss function for our program:

$$\lambda(d_1|\omega_1) = 0$$
$$\lambda(d_1|\omega_2) = 5$$
$$\lambda(d_2|\omega_1) = 10$$
$$\lambda(d_2|\omega_2) = 0$$

Now you can write the complete scripts for the program.

```
# decision action
# d1 = distribute water
# d2 = cleaning the water


# prior
p_w1 = 0.8
p_w2 = 0.2

# loss matrix
```

```
lambda_1_1 = 0
lambda_1_2 = 5
lambda_2_1 = 10
lambda_2_2 = 0


# class conditional probabilities
# taking some observations if water is bad or not.
# x1 = negative
# x2 = positive
p_x1_w1 = 0.3
p_x1_w2 = 0.7
p_x2_w1 = 0.2
p_x2_w2 = 0.8


# calculate p_x1 and p_x2
p_x1 = p_x1_w1 * p_w1 + p_x1_w2 * p_w2
p_x2 = p_x2_w1 * p_w1 + p_x2_w2 * p_w2


# calculate conditional risk given the observation
p_w1_x1 = (p_x1_w1 * p_w1) / p_x1
p_w2_x1 = (p_x1_w2 * p_w2) / p_x1
p_w1_x2 = (p_x2_w1 * p_w1) / p_x2
p_w2_x2 = (p_x2_w2 * p_w2) / p_x2


r_d1_x1 = p_w1_x1 * lambda_1_1 + p_w2_x1 * lambda_1_2
r_d2_x1 = p_w1_x1 * lambda_2_1 + p_w2_x1 * lambda_2_2
r_d1_x2 = p_w1_x2 * lambda_1_1 + p_w2_x2 * lambda_1_2
r_d2_x2 = p_w1_x2 * lambda_2_1 + p_w2_x2 * lambda_2_2

print("r_a1_x1: ", r_d1_x1)
print("r_a2_x1: ", r_d2_x1)
print("r_a1_x2: ", r_d1_x2)
print("r_a2_x2: ", r_d2_x2)


# calculate the total risk
e_d1 = p_x1 * r_d1_x1 + p_x2 * r_d1_x2
```

```
e_d2 = p_x1 * r_d2_x1 + p_x2 * r_d2_x2
print("e_d1: ", e_d1)
print("e_d2: ", e_d2)


if e_d1 < e_d2:
    print("final decision: d1 - distribute water")
else:
    print("final decision: d2 - cleaning the water")
```

Save the program into a file called `ch02_bayes_theory.py`. Then, run the program by typing this command:

```
$ python ch02_bayes_theory.py
```

You can see a sample of the program output in the following screenshot:

You can make more experiments by modifying prior and class conditional values.

Integrating a decision system and IoT project

IoT boards help us to perform sensing and actuating. To build a decision system with IoT boards, we can use a sensing process on IoT boards as input parameters for our decision system. After performing decision computing, we can make some actions through actuating on IoT boards.

In general, we can integrate our decision system with IoT boards, as shown in the following figure:

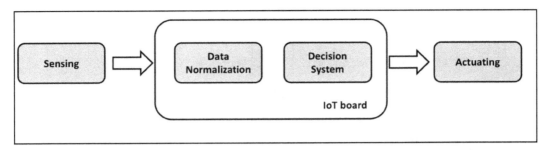

Several sensor devices can be attached to the IoT board that is used for sensing. Depending on what you need; you can gather environmental data, such as temperature, as digital inputs that will be used for our decision system. You can see samples of sensor devices in the following figure:

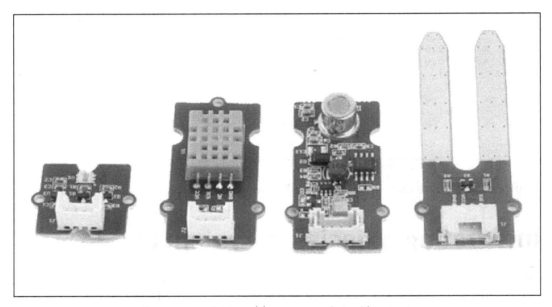

Image source: http://www.seeedstudio.com

Several actuator devices can be used in our decision system. Each final output from a system can be mapped into an action. This action can be represented as turning on an actuator device.

Some systems may not do sensing on their environment to gather input data. We can obtain data from a database or another system through a network.

Building your own decision system-based IoT

In this section, we build a simple decision system using fuzzy logic on Raspberry Pi. We use Python for implementation.

We build a system to monitor temperature and humidity in a room to decide if the environment is comfortable or not. If the environment is not comfortable, then we turn on a cooler machine.

The following is our design:

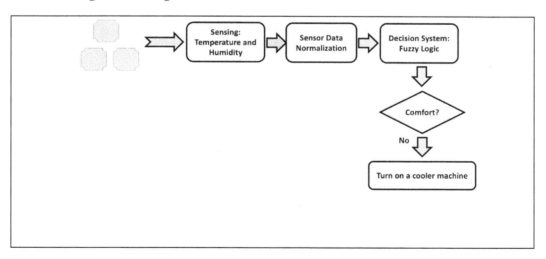

To sense temperature and humidity, we use the DHT22 module. We already learned about this module in *Chapter 1, Make Your IoT Project Smart*. A relay module is used to connect our Raspberry Pi to a cooler machine.

Let's start to build our system.

Wiring

We use DHT22 and relay modules for our wiring. Connect the DHT22 module into the following connections:

- DHT22 pin 1 (VDD) is connected to the 3.3V pin from Raspberry Pi
- DHT22 pin 2 (SIG) is connected to the GPIO23 (see the BCM column) pin from Raspberry Pi
- DHT22 pin 4 (GND) is connected to the GND pin from Raspberry Pi
- A relay VCC is connected to the 3.3V pin from Raspberry Pi
- A relay GND is connected to the GND pin from Raspberry Pi
- A relay signal is connected to the GPIO26 (see the BCM column) pin from Raspberry Pi

The complete wiring is shown in the following figure:

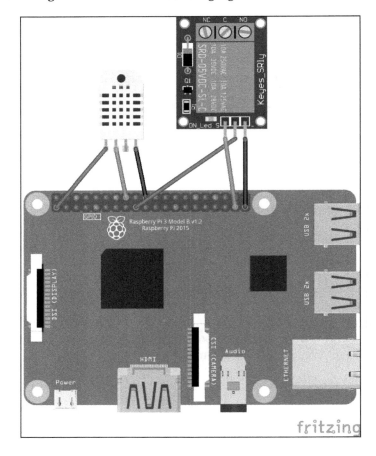

Writing the Python program

We build a fuzzy logic to implement a decision system. Two inputs from the sensing are temperature and humidity. In this case, we start developing a fuzzy membership for temperature and humidity.

For testing, I build the following fuzzy membership models for temperature and humidity, which are shown in the following screenshot:

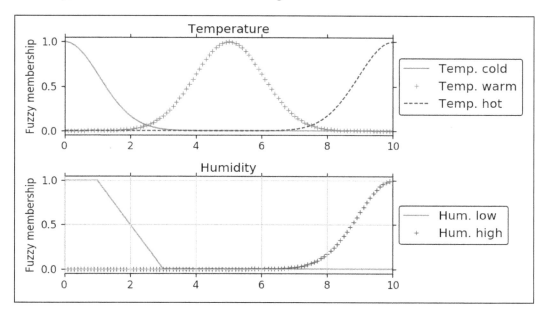

In the temperature model, we create three categories: cold, warm, and hot. Also, we make two categories for humidity: low and high.

Now we start to write the program. Firstly, create a file called ch02_fuzzy.py. Then, we initialize the required Python libraries:

```
import matplotlib
matplotlib.use('Agg')

import numpy as np
import skfuzzy as fuzz
import matplotlib.pyplot as plt

import Adafruit_DHT
import RPi.GPIO as GPIO
import time
```

After that, we initialize Raspberry Pi GPIO for DHT22 and relay module.

```
print('initialization...')

### initialization GPIO
relay_pin = 26
GPIO.setmode(GPIO.BCM)
GPIO.setup(relay_pin, GPIO.OUT)

sensor = Adafruit_DHT.DHT22
# DHT22 pin on Raspberry Pi
dht_pin = 23
```

The next step is to build a fuzzy logic model by starting to create fuzzy membership for temperature and humidity.

We create the `temperature_category()` and `humidity_category()` functions to map from sensing input to system.

```
######### INPUTS #####################
#Input Universe functions
temperature = np.arange(0, 11, 0.1)
humidity    = np.arange(0, 11, 0.1)

# Input Membership Functions
# Temperature
temperature_cold = fuzz.gaussmf(temperature, 0, 1.5)
temperature_warm = fuzz.gaussmf(temperature, 5, 1.5)
temperature_hot = fuzz.gaussmf(temperature, 10, 1.5)
# Humidity
humidity_low = fuzz.trapmf(humidity, [0, 0, 1, 3])
humidity_high = fuzz.gaussmf(humidity, 10, 1.5)

######### OUTPUT #####################
# comfort
# Output Variables Domain
comfort = np.arange(0, 30, 0.1)
# Output  Membership Function
comfort_low = fuzz.trimf(comfort, [0, 5, 10])
comfort_ave = fuzz.trimf(comfort, [10, 15, 25])
comfort_very = fuzz.trimf(comfort, [20, 25, 30])


def temperature_category(temperature_in=18):
```

```
    temperature_cat_cold = fuzz.interp_membership(temperature,
temperature_cold, temperature_in)
    temperature_cat_warm = fuzz.interp_membership(temperature,
temperature_warm, temperature_in)
    temperature_cat_hot = fuzz.interp_membership(temperature,
temperature_hot, temperature_in)
    return dict(cold=temperature_cat_cold, warm=temperature_cat_warm,
hot=temperature_cat_hot)


def humidity_category(humidity_in=2):
    humidity_cat_low = fuzz.interp_membership(humidity, humidity_low,
humidity_in)
    humidity_cat_high = fuzz.interp_membership(humidity, humidity_
high, humidity_in)
    return dict(low=humidity_cat_low, high=humidity_cat_high)
```

We also print our membership for reference into a file. It's done using a `matplotlib` library. We save fuzzy memberships for temperature and humidity.

```
# print membership
# Visualize these universes and membership functions
print('saving membership...')
fig, ax = plt.subplots(2, 1)

[t1, t2, t3] = ax[0].plot(temperature, temperature_cold, 'r',
temperature, temperature_warm, 'm+', temperature,
                          temperature_hot, 'b--', label=['Temp. cold',
'Temp. warm', 'Temp. hot'])
ax[0].set_ylabel('Fuzzy membership')
ax[0].set_title('Temperature')
ax[0].set_ylim(-0.05, 1.05)
ax[0].set_xlim(0, 10)

lgd1 = ax[0].legend([t1, t2, t3], ['Temp. cold', 'Temp. warm', 'Temp.
hot'], loc='center left', bbox_to_anchor=(1, 0.5))


[t1, t2] = ax[1].plot(humidity, humidity_low, 'r', humidity, humidity_
high, 'b+')
ax[1].set_ylabel('Fuzzy membership')
ax[1].set_title('Humidity')
ax[1].set_ylim(-0.05, 1.05)
ax[1].set_xlim(0, 10)
```

```
lgd2 = ax[1].legend([t1, t2], ['Hum. low', 'Hum. high'], loc='center
left', bbox_to_anchor=(1, 0.5))

plt.grid(True)
plt.tight_layout()
plt.show()
fig.savefig('fuzzy_mem_temp_hum.png', dpi=100, bbox_extra_
artists=(lgd1, lgd2, ), bbox_inches='tight')
print('done')
```

Now we are ready to read temperature and humidity via the DHT22 module. Then, compute them into our fuzzy logic system.

Furthermore, we make fuzzy inferences from our input data. We do fuzzy aggregation to generate the output.

The output is a numeric form. We can map it as low, average and very comfortable. From this situation, we can make a decision about whether we want to turn a cooler machine on or not:

```
# sensing and make decision
print('program is ready for making decision based fuzzy logic')
machine_state = -1
try:
    while 1:
        print('sensing...')
        sen_humidity, sen_temperature = Adafruit_DHT.read_
retry(sensor, dht_pin)

        if humidity is not None and temperature is not None:
            print('Sensing: Temperature={0:0.1f}*C
Humidity={1:0.1f}%'.format(sen_temperature, sen_humidity))

            sen_temperature = 18
            sen_humidity = 80
            # normalization
            norm_temperature = sen_temperature / 60.0
            norm_humidity = sen_humidity / 100.0
            print('Normalization: Temperature={0:0.0001f}
Humidity={1:0.0001f}'
                    .format(norm_temperature, norm_humidity))

            temp_in = temperature_category(norm_temperature)
            hum_in = humidity_category(norm_humidity)
```

```
            print('fuzzy membership: Temperature={0}  Humidity={1}'.
format(temp_in, hum_in))

            # Determine the weight and aggregate
            rule1 = np.fmax(temp_in['hot'], hum_in['low'])
            rule2 = temp_in['warm']
            rule3 = np.fmax(temp_in['warm'], hum_in['high'])

            imp1 = np.fmin(rule1, comfort_low)
            imp2 = np.fmin(rule2, comfort_ave)
            imp3 = np.fmin(rule3, comfort_very)

            aggregate_membership = np.fmax(imp1, imp2, imp3)

            # Defuzzify
            result_comfort = fuzz.defuzz(comfort, aggregate_
membership, 'centroid')
            print(result_comfort)

            # make decision based on experiment
            if result_comfort >= 5.002:
                if machine_state < 0:
                    machine_state = 1
                    print("turn on a machine")
                    GPIO.output(relay_pin, GPIO.HIGH)
                else:
                    print("a machine already turn on")
            else:
                if machine_state > 0:
                    machine_state = 0
                    print("turn off a machine")
                    GPIO.output(relay_pin, GPIO.LOW)
                else:
                    print("a machine already turn off")

            time.sleep(2)

        time.sleep(2)

except KeyboardInterrupt:
    GPIO.output(relay_pin, GPIO.LOW)
    GPIO.cleanup()


print('program is exit')
```

Save these scripts.

Testing

After we develop a program, we can start to run it. Type this command:

```
$ sudo python ch02_fuzzy.py
```

Make sure DHT22 and relay modules are already attached to Raspberry Pi. A sample program output is shown in the following screenshot:

```
●  ●  ●        Documents — pi@raspberrypi: ~/Documents/book — ssh pi@192.168.0.12 — 8...
pi@raspberrypi:~/Documents/book $ sudo python ch02_fuzzy.py
initialization...
saving membership...
done
program is ready for making decision based fuzzy logic
sensing...
Sensing: Temperature=28.6*C  Humidity=85.0%
Normalization: Temperature=0.3  Humidity=0.8
fuzzy membership: Temperature={'hot': 6.8987413995925987e-19, 'warm': 5.44745042
4466365e-05, 'cold': 0.96078943915232318}  Humidity={'high': 4.6005175273896544e
-17, 'low': 1.0}
5.00202884593
turn on a machine
sensing...
Sensing: Temperature=28.6*C  Humidity=85.1%
Normalization: Temperature=0.3  Humidity=0.8
fuzzy membership: Temperature={'hot': 6.8987413995925987e-19, 'warm': 5.44745042
4466365e-05, 'cold': 0.96078943915232318}  Humidity={'high': 4.6005175273896544e
-17, 'low': 1.0}
5.00202884593
a machine already turn on
sensing...
Sensing: Temperature=28.6*C  Humidity=85.0%
Normalization: Temperature=0.3  Humidity=0.8
fuzzy membership: Temperature={'hot': 6.8987413995925987e-19, 'warm': 5.44745042
4466365e-05, 'cold': 0.96078943915232318}  Humidity={'high': 4.6005175273896544e
-17, 'low': 1.0}
5.00202884593
a machine already turn on
sensing...
Sensing: Temperature=28.6*C  Humidity=85.1%
Normalization: Temperature=0.3  Humidity=0.8
fuzzy membership: Temperature={'hot': 6.8987413995925987e-19, 'warm': 5.44745042
```

Enhancement

This program is a sample of how to use fuzzy logic to develop a decision system. There are many ways you can improve this program. The following is an improvement area to which you can contribute:

- Modify the fuzzy membership model to improve the definition of comfort
- Add more input data to improve accuracy
- Add fuzzy inference methods to obtain the aggregation value

Summary

We have reviewed some basic decision systems by taking two samples, that is, Bayesian and fuzzy logic. We also explored Python libraries for implementing Bayesian and fuzzy logic and then practiced with them.

As the last topic, we deployed a decision system using fuzzy logic as a study sample on how to integrate a decision system on an IoT project with Raspberry Pi.

In the next chapter, we will learn how to build a vision machine for IoT project.

References

The following is a list of recommended books where you can learn more about the topics in this chapter.

1. Ethem Alpaydin. *Introduction to Machine Learning*. The MIT Press. 2004.

2. Peter D. Hoff. *A First Course in Bayesian Statistical Methods*. Springer, New York. 2009.

3. James V Stone. *Bayes' Rule: A Tutorial Introduction to Bayesian Analysis*. Sebtel Press. 2013.

4. Matt Sekerke. *Bayesian risk management: a guide to model risk and sequential learning in financial markets*. Wiley & Sons. 2015.

5. Timothy J. Ross. *Fuzzy logic with engineering applications, 3rd Edition*. John Wiley & Sons. 2010.

6. Hung T. Nguyen and Elbert A. Walker. *A First Course in Fuzzy Logic, 3rd Edition*. CRC Press. 2006.

3

Building Your
Own Machine Vision

Eyes are important for humans to see a beautiful world. In this chapter, we will explore how to make a machine see by deploying a camera. We will start to understand machine vision by detecting and tracking an object model by training our machine. Several camera modules will also be reviewed:

We explore the following topics:

- Introducing machine vision
- Introducing OpenCV library
- Deploying OpenCV library to Raspberry Pi
- Building a simple program with OpenCV
- Working with camera modules
- Introducing pattern recognition for machine vision
- Building a tracking vision system for moving objects
- Building your own IoT machine vision

Introducing machine vision

A machine vision is a machine with camera capabilities and an understanding of what objects are. The machine uses its camera to sense physical objects around its environment. Machine vision or computer vision is a field where a machine acquires, analyzes, and understands a still image or video. This field involves knowledge such as image processing, pattern recognition, and machine learning.

The pattern recognition and machine learning fields helps us to teach our machine to understand images. For instance, when we show a still image with people inside a car to the machine, then the machine should identify which are the people. Furthermore, in some cases, the machine also should guess the person in an image. From a pattern recognition and machine learning view, we should register the person so the machine can know the person in the image after identifying the person in an existing image.

To build a machine vision, we use the general design that is shown in the following figure:

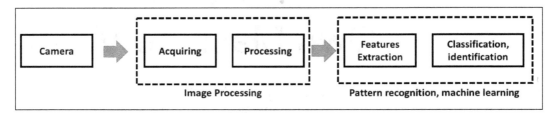

Firstly, we acquire image collection from a camera. Each image will be processed for image processing tasks such as removing noise, filtering or transforming. Then, we do feature extraction for each image.

There are various feature extraction techniques depending on your purposes. After obtaining the features of images, we identity and recognize objects in an image. Pattern recognition and machine learning take part in this process.

I won't explain more about pattern recognition and machine learning. I recommend you to read a textbook related to pattern recognition and machine learning. In this chapter, I'm going to show you how to achieve machine vision by applying pattern recognition and machine learning into IoT devices.

Introducing the OpenCV library

The **OpenCV (Open Computer Vision)** library is an open source library that is designed for computational efficiency and with a strong focus on real-time applications. This library is written in C/C++ and also provides several bindings for other programming languages. The official website for OpenCV is http://www. opencv.org.

The OpenCV library provides a complete library starting from basic computation and image processing to pattern recognition and machine learning. I notice several research papers use this library for simulation and experiments, so this library is a good point for starting our project in machine vision/computer vision.

Currently, the OpenCV library is available for Windows, Linux, Mac, Android and iOS. You can download this library at http://opencv.org/downloads.html. I'll show you how to deploy OpenCV on Raspberry Pi with Raspbian OS.

Deploying OpenCV on Raspberry Pi

In this section, we will deploy the OpenCV library on Raspberry Pi. I use Raspbian Jessie for testing. We're going to install OpenCV from source code in Raspberry Pi board.ss

Let's start to build the OpenCV library from source code on Raspberry Pi. Firstly, we install development libraries. Type these commands on the Raspberry Pi terminal:

```
$ sudo apt-get update
$ sudo apt-get install build-essential git cmake pkg-config libgtk2.0-dev
$ sudo apt-get install python2.7-dev python3-dev
```

We also need to install the required matrix, image and video libraries. You can type these commands:

```
$ sudo apt-get install libjpeg-dev libtiff5-dev libjasper-dev libpng12-dev
$ sudo apt-get install libavcodec-dev libavformat-dev libswscale-dev libv4l-dev
$ sudo apt-get install libxvidcore-dev libx264-dev
$ sudo apt-get install libatlas-base-dev gfortran
```

The next step is to download the OpenCV source code via Git. You can type these commands:

```
$ mkdir opencv
$ cd opencv
$ git clone https://github.com/Itseez/opencv.git
$ git clone https://github.com/Itseez/opencv_contrib.git
```

We use a Python virtual environment to deploy OpenCV on Raspberry Pi using virtualenv. The benefit of this approach is that it isolates our existing Python development environment.

If your Raspbian hasn't installed it yet, you can install it using `pip`.

```
$ sudo pip install virtualenv virtualenvwrapper
$ sudo rm -rf ~/.cache/pip
```

After that, you configure virtualenv in your bash profile:

```
$ nano ~/.profile
```

Then, add the following scripts:

```
export WORKON_HOME=$HOME/.virtualenvs
source /usr/local/bin/virtualenvwrapper.sh
```

Save your bash profile file if finished.

To create a Python virtual environment, you can type this command:

```
$ mkvirtualenv cv
```

This command will create a Python virtual environment, called `cv`.

If you use Python 3, you can create it with the following command:

```
$ mkvirtualenv cv -p python3
```

You should see (`cv`) on your terminal. If you close the terminal or call a new terminal, you should activate your Python virtual environment again. Type these commands:

```
$ source ~/.profile
$ workon cv
```

A sample of a form of Python virtual environment, called `cv`, can be seen in the following screenshot:

Inside Python virtual terminal, we continue to install NumPy as the required library for OpenCV Python. We can install this library using `pip`.

```
$ pip install numpy
```

Now we're ready to build and install OpenCV from source. After cloning the OpenCV library, you can build it by typing the following commands:

```
$ cd ~/opencv/
$ mkdir build
$ cd build
$ cmake -D CMAKE_BUILD_TYPE=RELEASE \
  -D CMAKE_INSTALL_PREFIX=/usr/local \
  -D INSTALL_C_EXAMPLES=ON \
  -D INSTALL_PYTHON_EXAMPLES=ON \
  -D OPENCV_EXTRA_MODULES_PATH=~/opencv/opencv_contrib/modules \
  -D BUILD_EXAMPLES=ON ..
```

Furthermore, we install the OpenCV library on our internal system from Raspbian OS.

```
$ make -j4
$ sudo make install
$ sudo ldconfig
```

If done, we should configure the library so Python can access it through Python binding. The following is a list of command steps for configuring with Python 2.7:

```
$ ls -1 /usr/local/lib/python2.7/site-packages/
$ cd ~/.virtualenvs/cv/lib/python2.7/site-packages/
$ ln -s /usr/local/lib/python2.7/site-packages/cv2.so cv2.so
```

If you use Python 3.x, for instance Python 3.4, you do the following steps on the terminal. Consider if you use Python 3.4.x:

```
$ ls /usr/local/lib/python3.4/site-packages/
$ cd /usr/local/lib/python3.4/site-packages/
$ sudo mv cv2.cpython-34m.so cv2.so
$ cd ~/.virtualenvs/cv/lib/python3.4/site-packages/
$ ln -s /usr/local/lib/python3.4/site-packages/cv2.so cv2.so
```

The installation process is over. Now we need to verify whether our OpenCV installation is correct by checking the OpenCV version.

```
$ workon cv
$ python
>>> import cv2
>>> cv2.__version__
```

You should see the OpenCV version on the terminal. A sample of program output is shown in the following screenshot:

```
● ● ●   ⌂  agusk — pi@raspberrypi: ~/opencv — ssh pi@192.168.0.12 — 80×21
(cv) pi@raspberrypi:~/opencv $ python
Python 2.7.9 (default, Mar  8 2015, 00:52:26)
[GCC 4.9.2] on linux2
Type "help", "copyright", "credits" or "license" for more information.
>>> import cv2
>>> cv2.__version__
'3.1.0-dev'
>>>
```

The next demo displays an image file using OpenCV. For this scenario, we can use the cv2.imshow() function to display a picture file.

For testing, log into the Raspberry Pi desktop to execute the program. Using a text editor, you can type the following scripts:

```
import numpy as np
import cv2


img = cv2.imread('circle.png')
cv2.imshow('My photo', img)
cv2.waitKey(0)
cv2.destroyAllWindows()
```

I use `circle.png` file as a picture source. You can find it in this book's source codes. Save these scripts into a file called `ch03_hello_opencv.py`. Then, open the terminal inside your Raspberry Pi desktop and type this command:

```
$ python ch03_hello_opencv.py
```

If successful, you should see a dialog that displays a picture:

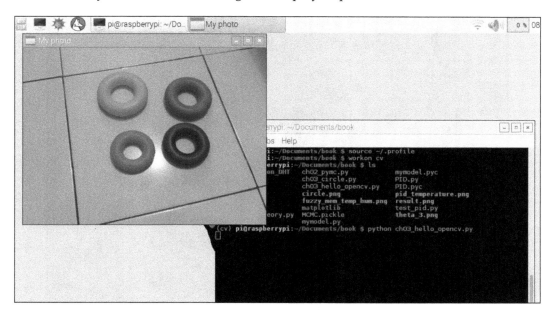

The picture dialog shows up because we called `cv2.waitKey(0)` in our code. Press any key on the picture dialog if you want to close the dialog.

After received a clicked key event, we close the dialog by calling the `cv2.destroyAllWindows()` function.

Building a simple program with OpenCV

There are many program samples that show how to use OpenCV using Python. In our case, we build a simple program to detect a circle in a still image.

Consider we have the following image, which is used for testing. You can find the image file in the source code files, called `circle.png`.

To find a circle in a still image, we use **circle Hough Transform (CHT)**. A circle can be defined as follows:

$$(x - a)^2 + (y - b)^2 = r^{2}$$

(a,b) is the center of a circle with radius *r*. These parameters will be computed using the CHT method.

Let's build a demo!

We will build a program to read an image file. Then, we will detect a circle form in an image using the `cv2.HoughCircles()` function.

Let's start to write these scripts:

```
import cv2
import numpy as np


print('load image')
orig = cv2.imread('circle.png')
processed = cv2.imread('circle.png', 0)
processed = cv2.medianBlur(processed, 19)

print('processing...')
circles = cv2.HoughCircles(processed, cv2.HOUGH_GRADIENT, 1, 70,
                param1=30,
                param2=15,
                minRadius=0,
                maxRadius=50)


circles = np.uint16(np.around(circles))
for (x, y, r) in circles[0, :]:
    cv2.circle(orig, (x, y), r, (0, 255, 0), 2)

print('completed')
print('writing to a file..')
cv2.imwrite('circle_process.png', orig)
print('done')
```

Save these scripts into a file called `ch03_circle.py`.

To run the program, type this command on the Raspberry Pi terminal:

```
$ python ch03_circle.py
```

Make sure `circle.png` and `ch03_circle.py` are located in the same folder.

You should see some text on the terminal. You can see the sample of program output in the following screenshot:

```
agusk — pi@raspberrypi: ~/Documents/book — ssh pi@192.168.0.12 — 80×21
(cv) pi@raspberrypi:~/Documents/book $ ls
Adafruit_Python_DHT     ch02_pymc.py            mymodel.pyc
alpha.png               ch03_circle.py          PID.py
beta.png                ch03_hello_opencv.py    PID.pyc
ch01_dht22.py           circle.png              pid_temperature.png
ch01_led.py             fuzzy_mem_temp_hum.png  result.png
ch01_pid.py             matplotlib              test_pid.py
ch02_bayes_theory.py    MCMC.pickle             theta_3.png
ch02_fuzzy.py           mymodel.py
(cv) pi@raspberrypi:~/Documents/book $ python ch03_circle.py
load image
processing...
completed
writing to a file..
done
(cv) pi@raspberrypi:~/Documents/book $
```

This program will detect a circle form in an image file. After finishing the detection process, the program will generate a new image file, called `circle_process.png`.

If you open `circle_process.png` file, you should see four circle drawings in the image file, shown in the following figure:

How does it work?

Firstly, we load OpenCV and NumPy libraries into our program:

```
import cv2
import numpy as np
```

We read the image file using `cv2.imread()` into two variables, `orig` and `processed`. The `processed` variable is used to manipulate to find a circle. The image in `processed` variable will changed due to the blurring process.

```
orig = cv2.imread('circle.png')
processed = cv2.imread('circle.png', 0)
processed = cv2.medianBlur(processed, 19)
```

`cv2.medianBlue()` is used to blur an image by defining a median value. The parameter value should be an odd value, such as 1, 3, 5, 7.

To find circles in an image, we can use `cv2.HoughCircles()`. `param1` and `param2` values, which are defined based on this paper `http://www.bmva.org/bmvc/1989/avc-89-029.pdf`.

```
circles = cv2.HoughCircles(processed, cv2.HOUGH_GRADIENT, 1, 70,
                param1=30,
                param2=15,
                minRadius=0,
                maxRadius=50)
```

Draw all circles found on the original image, the `orig` variable:

```
circles = np.uint16(np.around(circles))
for (x, y, r) in circles[0, :]:
    cv2.circle(orig, (x, y), r, (0, 255, 0), 2)
```

The last step is to save our computation result into a file called `circle_process.png`, using `cv2.imwrite()`:

```
cv2.imwrite('circle_process.png', orig)
```

Working with camera modules

In this section, we explore various camera modules for the Raspberry Pi board. There are many camera models that fit your projects. Camera modules can be reviewed based on what kind of Raspberry Pi interface is used to attach the modules.

Let's explore.

Camera modules based on the CSI interface

The Raspberry Pi camera is the official camera board released by the Raspberry Pi Foundation. This camera can be attached to the Raspberry Pi board through the CSI interface. The Raspberry Pi Foundation also provides another camera model, the Raspberry Pi NoIR Camera. This can work in low light (twilight) environments. A form of Raspberry Pi Camera v2 and NoIR camera v2 can been seen in the following figure:

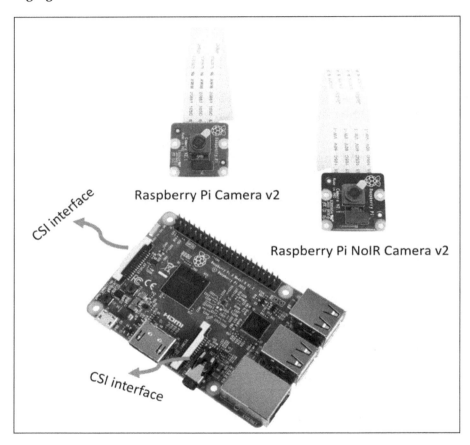

These modules are official camera devices for Raspberry Pi. To use a camera over the CSI interface, we should enable it on Raspbian. You can configure it using the `raspi-config` tool. Just type command on the Raspberry Pi terminal.

```
$ sudo raspi-config
```

After execution, you should see the `raspi-config` program, which is shown in the following screenshot:

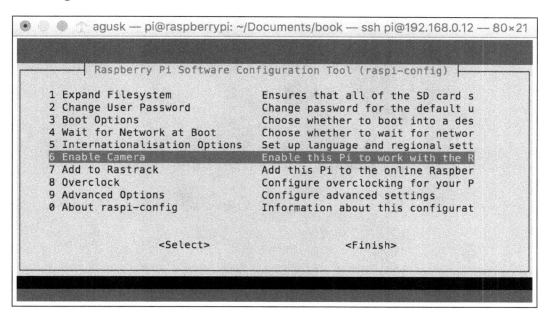

Select the **6 Enable Camera** option on the `raspi-config` tool. Then, click on **Enable Camera** to activate the camera modules. If finished, you should be asked to restart Raspbian. Restart Raspbian to complete the changed configuration.

Now you can use this camera with your program.

Camera modules based on USB interface

Camera modules with a USB interface are common camera devices. This device is usually called a webcam. You can easily find them in your local stores.

Image source: `http://www.amazon.com/Microsoft-LifeCam-Cinema-Webcam-Business/dp/B004ABQAFO/`

A camera module with USB can be attached to the Raspberry Pi board through the USB. For Raspberry Pi 3, you have four USB adapters, so you can attach four camera modules based on USB.

Several camera module-based USBs can be recognized by Raspberry Pi including the OpenCV library. You can find compatible USB webcams for Raspberry Pi on this site, `http://elinux.org/RPi_USB_Webcams`.

Camera modules-based serial interface

If your IoT boards don't have a USB interface but do have UART/serial pins, you can use a camera modules-based serial interface. The Grove-Serial Camera kit is one of these, which is shown in the following figure:

Image source: http://www.seeedstudio.com/item_detail.html?p_id=1608

A camera module with UART interface can be attached to Raspberry Pi boards through UART GPIO pins.

Camera modules with multi-interfaces

I found several camera module devices with multi-interfaces that support serial, USB, SPI and I2C interfaces. This is a good point, because we can attach them in our favorite boards.

Pixy CMUcam is one of the camera modules with a multi-interface. You can read and buy this module on the official website, http://cmucam.org. Some online stores also sell this module. I got Pixy CMUcam5 board and pan/tilt module from SeeedStudio, http://www.seeedstudio.com.

I'm going to share how to use the Pixy CMUcam5 module with a Raspberry Pi board in the last section.

Accessing camera modules from the OpenCV library

In the previous section, we used a still image as a source for the OpenCV library. We can use a camera as the source of a still image. A camera generates video data, which is a collection of still images. To access camera modules from the OpenCV library, follow these steps:

1. To access a camera from OpenCV, we can use the `VideoCapture` object. We call `read()` to read a frame, which is a still of a frame.

2. For a demo, we use the camera USB drive. Just connect this device to the Raspberry Pi board through the USB drive. Then, we write the following scripts with your text editor:

```
import numpy as np
import cv2


cap = cv2.VideoCapture(0)
while True:
    # Capture frame-by-frame
    ret, frame = cap.read()

    # Display the resulting frame
    cv2.imshow('video player', frame)
    if cv2.waitKey(1) & 0xFF == ord('q'):
        break


cap.release()
cv2.destroyAllWindows()
```

3. Save these scripts into a file, called `ch03_camera_player.py`.

4. To run this program, you should enter the Python virtual environment, which already deployed the OpenCV library.

5. Type this command:

```
$ python ch03_camera_player.py
```

6. If you succeed, you will have a dialog that shows streaming video from a camera. A sample of program output can be seen in the following screenshot:

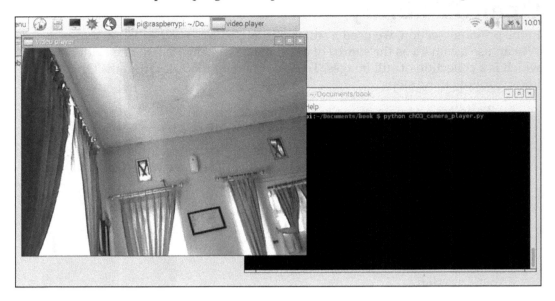

7. To exit or close the dialog, you can press a key *Q*.

8. If you see the function, `cv2.VideoCapture(0)`, call the attached camera. If you attached more than one camera, call `cv2.VideoCapture(1)` for the second camera.

Introducing pattern recognition for machine vision

Pattern recognition is an important part of machine vision or computer vision, to teach a machine to understand the object in an image.

In this section, we explore a paper by Paul Viola and Michael Jones about *Rapid Object Detection using a Boosted Cascade of Simple Features*. This paper describes a machine learning approach for visual object detection.

In general, the Viola and Jones approach is known as Haar Cascades. Their algorithm uses AdaBoost algorithm with the following classifier:

$$h(x) = \begin{cases} 1 & \sum_{t=1}^{T} \alpha_t h_t(x) \geq \frac{1}{2} \sum_{t=1}^{T} \alpha_t \\ 0 & otherwise \end{cases}$$

Fortunately, the OpenCV library has implemented Viola and Jones' approach to visual object detection. Other people also contributed to data training from Haar Cascades. You can find training data files on the OpenCV source code, which is located on <opencv_source_codes>/data/haarcascades/.

You can now test detection of faces on an image using the Haar Cascades approach. You can write the following scripts:

```
import numpy as np
import cv2


face_cascade = cv2.CascadeClassifier('haarcascade_frontalface_default.
xml')

img = cv2.imread('children.png')
gray = cv2.cvtColor(img, cv2.COLOR_BGR2GRAY)

faces = face_cascade.detectMultiScale(gray, 1.3, 5)
for (x, y, w, h) in faces:
    img = cv2.rectangle(img, (x, y), (x+w, y+h), (0, 255, 255), 2)


cv2.imshow('img', img)
cv2.waitKey(0)
cv2.destroyAllWindows()
```

Save these scripts into a file called ch03_faces.py.

You also put files, haarcascade_frontalface_default.xml and children.png, on the same path with the program. The haarcascade_frontalface_default.xml file can be obtained from the <opencv_source_codes>/data/haarcascades/ and children.png file is taken from the source code of this book.

Run this program on the terminal with the Raspberry Pi desktop by typing this command:

```
$ python ch03_faces.py
```

After running, you should get a dialog with a picture. There are three faces detected, but one is missing. In my opinion, Haar Cascades approach is still good even it's not the best method. A sample of program output can be seen in the following screenshot:

How does it work?

Firstly, we load the required libraries and training data for Haar Cascades:

```
import numpy as np
import cv2
face_cascade = cv2.CascadeClassifier('haarcascade_frontalface_default.
xml')
```

We load a picture file for testing and then change the image color to gray:

```
img = cv2.imread('children.png')
gray = cv2.cvtColor(img, cv2.COLOR_BGR2GRAY)
```

To detect a face, we call `face_cascade.detectMultiScale()` with passing image vector, scale factor and minimum neighbors. If a detected face is found, we draw a rectangle on the picture:

```
faces = face_cascade.detectMultiScale(gray, 1.3, 5)
for (x, y, w, h) in faces:
    img = cv2.rectangle(img, (x, y), (x+w, y+h), (0, 255, 255), 2)
```

The last step is to show a picture and wait pressed key. If any key is pressed, a picture dialog is closed.

```
cv2.imshow('img', img)
cv2.waitKey(0)
cv2.destroyAllWindows()
```

Building a tracking vision system for moving objects

In this section, we build a simple tacking vision system. We already learned how to detect a face in an image. Now we try to detect faces on video.

The idea is simple. We change a still image as source to a frame image from a camera. After calling `read()` from the `VideoCapture` object, we pass the frame image into `face_cascade.detectMultiScale()`. Then, we show it a picture dialog. That's it.

For implementation, type these scripts:

```
import numpy as np
import cv2

face_cascade = cv2.CascadeClassifier('haarcascade_frontalface_default.
xml')
cap = cv2.VideoCapture(0)
while True:
    # Capture frame-by-frame
    ret, frame = cap.read()

    gray = cv2.cvtColor(frame, cv2.COLOR_BGR2GRAY)

    faces = face_cascade.detectMultiScale(gray, 1.3, 5)
    for (x, y, w, h) in faces:
        img = cv2.rectangle(frame, (x, y), (x + w, y + h), (0, 255,
255), 2)

    cv2.imshow('face tracking', frame)
```

```
    if cv2.waitKey(1) & 0xFF == ord('q'):
        break


cap.release()
cv2.destroyAllWindows()
```

Save this program into a file called ch03_faces_camera.py.

Now you can run this program on the terminal from the Raspberry Pi desktop.

```
$ python ch03_faces_camera.py
```

After running, try to show your face. Then, the program should detect your face. You can see the program output in the following figure:

You can modify this project by adding an LED as an indicator for which a face is already detected.

How does it work?

This program runs as the previous program. We only change the image source from the camera.

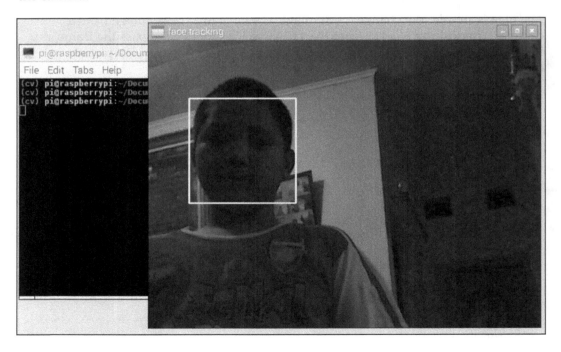

Building your own IoT machine vision

We already know Pixy CMUcam5 as a camera module. In this section, we try to use this module in our IoT project.

The following is a list of the required modules:

- Pixy CMUcam5 Sensor, `http://www.seeedstudio.com/item_detail.html?p_id=2048`
- Pan/Tilt for Pixy, `http://www.seeedstudio.com/item_detail.html?p_id=2048`

You also can obtain these modules on other online stores.

Deploying Pixy CMUcam5 on Raspberry Pi

In order to use Pixy CMUcam5, you should install the required libraries and applications. Firstly, you can open the terminal on Raspberry Pi and type these commands:

```
$ sudo apt-get install libusb-1.0-0-dev
$ sudo apt-get install qt4-dev-tools
$ sudo apt-get install qt4-qmake qt4-default
$ sudo apt-get install g++
$ sudo apt-get install swig
$ sudo apt-get install libboost-all-dev
```

You need the Pixy library and application from source code. Firstly, you download the source code and then install PixyMon:

```
$ git clone https://github.com/charmedlabs/pixy.git
$ cd pixy/scripts
$ ./build_pixymon_src.sh
```

In order to use the Pixy library from Python, you can install Python binding. Type this command on the path `<pixy_library>/pixy/scripts`:

```
$./build_libpixyusb_swig.sh
```

You need to configure to access Pixy over USB without a non-root user. Type these commands:

```
$ cd ../src/host/linux/
$ sudo cp pixy.rules /etc/udev/rules.d/
```

Now you're ready to use Pixy CMUcam5.

Assembly

To setup Pixy CMUcam5 and Pan/Tilt, I recommend you read this guideline,
http://cmucam.org/projects/cmucam5/wiki/Assembling_pantilt_Mechanism.
The following is my assembly, shown in the following figure:

Updating the Pixy CMUcam5 firmware

Before you use the Pixy CMUcam5 module, I recommend you update the board
firmware. You can download it on http://cmucam.org/projects/cmucam5/wiki/
Latest_release. For instance, you can download Pixy firmware 2.0.19 directly on
http://cmucam.org/attachments/download/1317/pixy_firmware-2.0.19-
general.hex.

To update the firmware, you should run the PoxyMon application. Please unplug the
Pixy CMUcam5 from Raspberry Pi. Then, press the white button on the top of the
Pixy CMUcam5 board and plug the board in to Raspberry Pi through the USB. Please
keep pressing the white button until you get a folder dialog. Then release the white
button on Pixy CMUcam5, and select the Pixy firmware file. Wait until the flashing
firmware is done.

Testing

We start to test Pixy CMUcam5 with Raspberry Pi. Several demos are provided to show how Pixy CMUcam5 works. Let's start!

Loading streaming video

After we have deployed the Pixy CMUcam5 application and library, we will obtain the PixyMon application. It's a tool to manage our training data and can be found on `<pixy_codes>/build/pixymon/bin/`.

Navigate to `<pixy_codes>/build/pixymon/bin/`, then type this command on the terminal with Raspberry Pi in desktop mode.

```
$ ./PixyMon
```

If done correctly, you should see a **PixyMon** dialog, shown in the following screenshot:

If you don't see any picture on the dialog, you can click the red circle icon, which is shown by the arrow. This puts the PixyMon application in streaming video mode. The following screenshot is a sample of my program output:

Tracking an object

Pixy CMUcam5 can track any object after the object is already registered. In this section, we explore how to register a new object and then track it.

1. Plug Pixy CMUcam5 into the Raspberry Pi board. Open the **PixyMon** application. Show it any object you want to track.

2. Keep your target object on the camera. Then, click menu **Action | Set signature 1** on the PixyMon application.

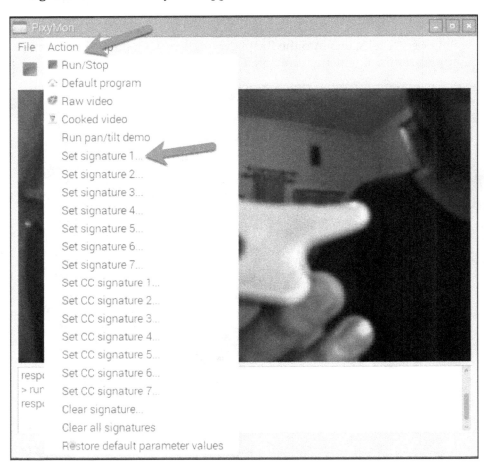

3. This makes PixyMon freeze the image so you can set a region of your target object using a mouse:

4. After that, PixyMon saves the signature data. Then, the application will track your object. Move your target object.

Tracking an object with a Pan/Tilt module

If you have a Pan/Tilt module already attached to Pixy CMUcam5, you can play a demo to track the object through Pan/Tilt.

1. Using your registered signature, you can activate **Pan/Tilt** by clicking menu **Action | Run Pan/Tilt demo** on the PixyMon application.

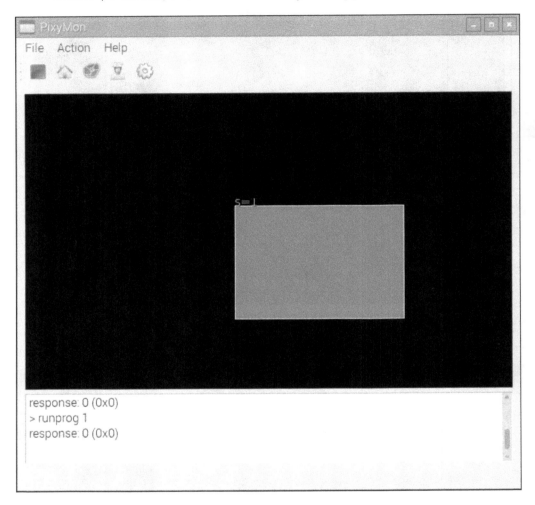

2. Try to move your target object. The Pan/Tilt module will move to where the target object is located.

Running the Python application

Using the same registered signature, we can get a signature position. We can use a sample program written in Python.

You can find `get_blocks.py` file in the folder `<pixy_codes>/build/libpixyusb_swig/`. After that, you can add this file:

```
$ python get_blocks.py
```

The program will acquire the position of the signature if it's found. You can see the program output in the following screenshot:

```
● ● ●    agusk — pi@raspberrypi: ~/pixy/pixy/build/libpixyusb_swig — ssh pi@192.168....
[pi@raspberrypi:~/pixy/pixy/scripts $ ls
build_hello_pixy.sh          build_pantilt_c_demo.sh       install_libpixyusb.sh
build_libpixyusb.sh          build_pantilt_python_demo.sh  pack_pixymon_src.sh
build_libpixyusb_swig.sh  build_pixymon_src.sh
[pi@raspberrypi:~/pixy/pixy/scripts $ cd ..
pi@raspberrypi:~/pixy/pixy $ cd build/
libpixyusb/        libpixyusb_swig/ pixymon/
[pi@raspberrypi:~/pixy/pixy $ cd build/libpixyusb_swig/
[pi@raspberrypi:~/pixy/pixy/build/libpixyusb_swig $ ls
build  get_blocks.py  pixy.i  pixy.py  _pixy.so  pixy_wrap.cxx  setup.py  src
[pi@raspberrypi:~/pixy/pixy/build/libpixyusb_swig $ python get_blocks.py
Pixy Python SWIG Example -- Get Blocks
frame    0:
[BLOCK_TYPE=0 SIG=1 X=309 Y=198 WIDTH=  9 HEIGHT=  2]
frame    1:
[BLOCK_TYPE=0 SIG=1 X=309 Y=198 WIDTH=  9 HEIGHT=  2]
frame    2:
[BLOCK_TYPE=0 SIG=1 X=309 Y=198 WIDTH=  9 HEIGHT=  2]
frame    3:
[BLOCK_TYPE=0 SIG=1 X=309 Y=198 WIDTH=  9 HEIGHT=  2]
```

What's next?

You can modify the program to control Pixy CMUcam5 module with the Raspberry Pi board.

Clearing all signatures

If you have finished all experiments and don't want to use signature data again, you can clear them by clicking menu **Action** | **Clear all signatures** on PixyMon application.

Summary

We have learned some basic machine vision using OpenCV. We also explored Python to access OpenCV and then practiced with them.

As the last topic, we deployed machine vision on a Raspberry Pi board to build face detection and track an object.

In the next chapter, we will learn how to build an autonomous car using machine learning.

References

The following is a list of recommended books where you can learn more about the topics in this chapter.

1. Richard Szeliski. Computer Vision: *Algorithms and Applications*, Springer. 2011.

2. P. Viola and M. Jones, *Rapid object detection using a boosted cascade of simple features*, Computer Vision and Pattern Recognition, 2001. CVPR 2001. Proceedings of the 2001 IEEE Computer Society Conference on, 2001, pp. I-511-I-518 vol. 1.

3. OpenCV library, `http://opencv.org`.

4
Making Your Own Autonomous Car Robot

In this chapter, we will explore how to build a car robot by integrating some sensor and actuator devices to make the robot run without human interference. We will also learn how to navigate the robot and control it from your computer.

We will explore the topics in the following sections:

- Introducing autonomous systems
- Introducing mobile robots
- Building your own car robot
- Working with the Pololu Zumo robot for Arduino
- Controlling a car robot from a computer
- Working with a GPS module for navigation
- Introducing map engine platforms
- Building a navigated car-based GPS
- Making your own autonomous car

Introducing autonomous systems

An autonomous system is a system that performs something automatically by self-learning. In traditional systems, we define a to-do list on the system. Then, the system runs and performs something in accordance with its to-do list. In terms of an autonomous system, we can make a system learn itself.

In the field of robot study, there are two basic problems in autonomous robotic systems:

- The path- and motion-planning problem
- The motion control problem

The path- and motion-planning problem describes which path is taken by the robot to move from one point to another point. In robot movement, the robot can move with or without a map. The motion control problem shows how our robot moves. It can be a maze or a zigzag from one point to another point.

In general, an autonomous system architecture can be designed as shown in the following figure:

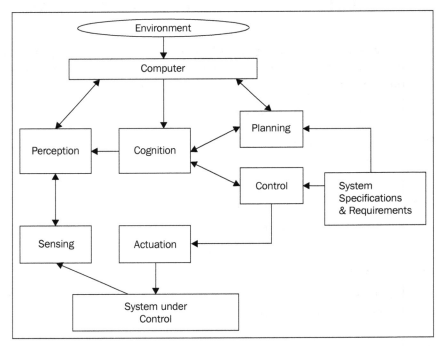

Source image: Meystel, A.: Intelligent Control: A Sketch of the Theory, 1. Intelligent and Robotic Systems, Vol. 2, 1989, pp. 97-107.

In the preceding figure, we can see six key elements needed to build an autonomous system:

- Cognition
- Perception
- Planning
- Control
- Sensing
- Actuation

In this chapter, we will learn how to implement the key elements of autonomous systems. We use the existing robot platform and Arduino board to deploy the autonomous robot.

Introducing mobile robots

A mobile robot is a robot with the capacity to move. It has motors to get moving from one point to another point. In general, we can build a mobile robot using the five components that are described in the following figure:

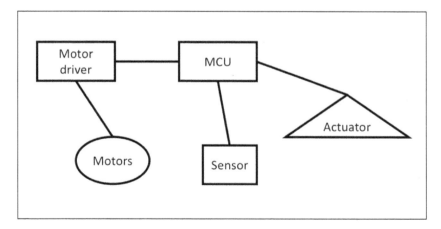

MCU (Microprocessor Central Unit) is the command central of our robot. It can be an Arduino, Intel Edison, BeagleBone Black/Green, or Raspberry Pi board. Each MCU board has unique capabilities, as well as being programmable. You might need to select an MCU board model by referring to its size and weight, depending on your needs.

Depending on how your robot will move, you can use any motor model. To control motors, we need a motor driver because some MCUs may not have PWM/Analog outputs. In addition, motors usually need higher voltage. If we connect the MCU and motors directly, they may get a broken connection on your MCU. A motor driver module usually has a voltage regulator to control power usage in motors.

To gather information from robot's environment, we need sensor modules. A sensor module has the capability of capturing physical input, and then convert to digital data. There are many sensor devices that can be attached to your MCU. Each sensor module has unique output data as result of sensing environmental inputs such as temperature or humidity. A camera can be a sensor module, functioning as an optical sensor that can capture the robot's environment.

A robot also needs to be able to interact with its environment. It does this via actuators. An LED is a simple actuator that is used to indicate specific information. For instance, a robot with a gas sensor detects a dangerous gas, so another robot turns on a red LED as a warning signal. You can use some actuators with your robot platform, but you should be aware of the limitations of the battery that powers your actuator.

Building your own car robot

In this section, we will build a car robot. There are many options to implement your own robot. The following is a checklist of features that you may wish to consider when designing your car robot:

- **Objective**: What kind of goals do you want to achieve in building a car robot? Just for fun, or research, or for a professional project?

- **MCU**: What level of complexity will be involved in programming your robot? Is it enough to use an Arduino board, or would you need a complex MCU board, such as Raspberry Pi?

- **Battery**: This is very important. You can choose battery models depending on the power lifespan that you require.

- **Sensors and actuators**: Please use the appropriate sensors and actuators with your robot board. More sensors and actuators means you need more battery power. This also impacts on your robot's weight.

You should draw up another checklist dealing with your robot's performance.

In the next section, we will review the two categories of robot platforms: DIY robot platforms and assembled robot platforms.

DIY robot platforms

DIY (Do-It-Yourself) robot platforms require and allow more creativity in building a robot. Several robot vendors usually sell all required parts of a robot kit. With this platform, you have the sole responsibility of building your own robot, included soldering electronics components.

SparkFun Inventor's Kit for RedBot, `https://www.sparkfun.com/products/12649`, is a sample of a DIY robot platform.

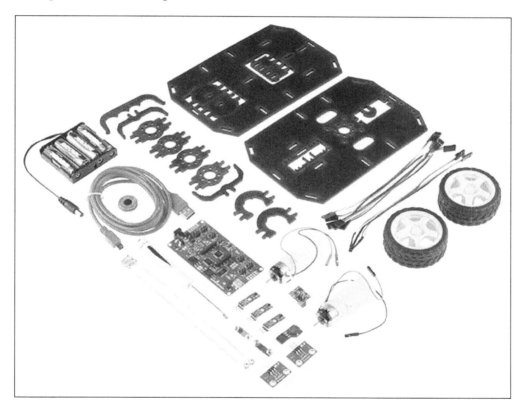

SparkFun Inventor's Kit for RedBot is a completed robot. You need to assemble all parts to build a mobile robot. This kit includes an MCU board based on the Arduino model so you can write programs easily.

I also found a cheap DIY robot platform from a Chinese manufacturer, namely DIY Smart Motor Robot Car, from Banggood (`http://www.banggood.com/DIY-Smart-Motor-Robot-Car-Chassis-Battery-Box-Kit-Speed-Encoder-For-Arduino-p-1044541.html`). You also buy it on `dx.com`, eBay, AliExpress, and Alibaba.

DIY Smart Motor Robot Car kit does not come with an MCU board, so you'll have to buy an MCU board, such as Arduino or Raspberry Pi, separately. Once you get this kit, you can build a robot car by following the instructions.

I am sure there are many DIY kits in your local store with which you can build a robot. Please be creative!

Assembled robot platform

If you are too lazy to build a robot, or don't want to solder electronic parts, you can buy an assembled robot kit. You can focus on writing programs on the robot instead of building it from scratch. Some robot vendors sell assembled robot kits. Choose your robot platform, the including the programming model. For instance, if you want to write robot programs based on the Arduino platform, then you can use Pololu Zumo Arduino, `https://www.pololu.com/product/2510`.

Zumo Robot for Arduino is designed as an Arduino shield, which is supported for Arduino Uno model. You also use Arduino Leonardo, Arduino 101, and Arduino Zero. Please make sure your Arduino pin power works on 5V.

Alternatively, we can use Zumo 32U4 Robot from Pololu, found at `https://www.pololu.com/product/3125`. In this model, we don't need an Arduino board because Zumo 32U4 Robot has already been constructed with an Arduino board inside. We just write a Sketch program and then deploy it into the board.

Another option is Makeblock mBot V1.1 from Makeblock, found at `http://makeblock.com/mbot-v1-1-stem-educational-robot-kit`. This kit has a completed robot that is based on Arduino Uno. There are two robot kit models that you can choose based on the communication model. Makeblock mBot V1.1 provides Bluetooth and radio as their wireless module stack. You can select the wireless module when you buy this kit.

To build a program for Makeblock mBot, Makeblock provides a development tool, called mBlock. It is a custom build based on Scratch (`https://scratch.mit.edu`). You can draw a program by clicking and dragging.

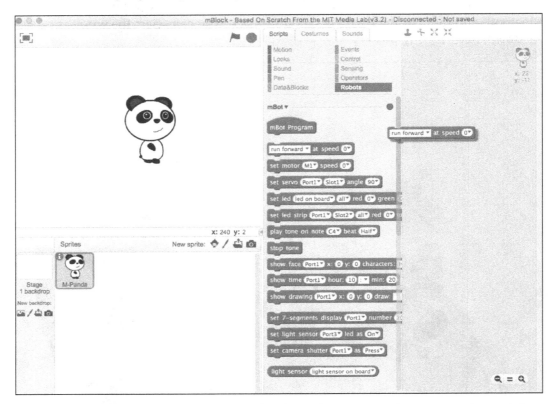

Source: `http://learn.makeblock.com/en/getting-started-programming-with-mblock/`

Working with the Pololu Zumo robot for Arduino

In this section, we will make a simple robot with simple movements based on avoiding obstacles. If the robot faces an obstacle, the robot will turn left to avoid it. To make this happen, we can use an Ultrasonic module to detect an obstacle.

I usually use HC-SR04 as an Ultrasonic module. It's cheap, and you can buy it on dx.com, banggood.com, and AliExpress. You can see the HC-SR04 module form in the following figure:

The HC-SR04 module provides four pins: VCC, GND, Trigger, and Echo. You can connect Trigger and Echo pins to Arduino digital I/O. But how can you connect the HC-SR04 module into Pololu Zumo robot for Arduino?

Based on the user guide from Pololu, you can connect them through Arduino digital I/O on pins 4, 11, 5, 2. The easier way is to connect HC-SR04 module via the front expansion pins. You can see this in the following figure:

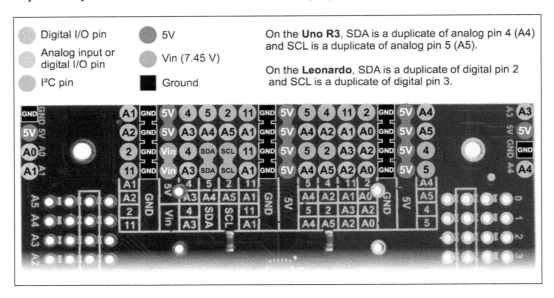

For our demo wiring, connect Trigger and Echo pins to Arduino digital I/O on pins 2 and 4. The VCC and GND pins of Ultrasonic module are connected to 5V and GND pins on Arduino. The following is our demo wiring:

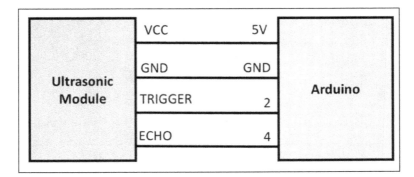

Another option that you might try is to connect the Ultrasonic module from Pololu Zumo robot shield plate by soldering it with the pin header. Just make sure you use digital pins 4, 11, 5 and 2 because these pins aren't used by Pololu Zumo robot shield.

The following figure is a sample of my wiring implementation:

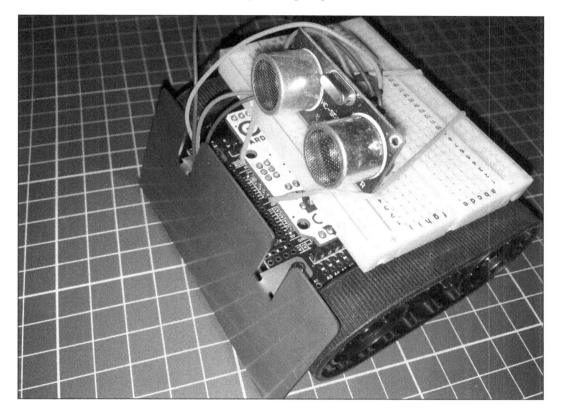

We will use the NewPing library on our Sketch program. You can download it from http://playground.arduino.cc/Code/NewPing and then deploy it into the Arduino libraries folder. After it has been deployed, you can start to write the Sketch program.

Open Arduino IDE and write the following code:

```
#include <NewPing.h>
#include <ZumoMotors.h>

#define TRIGGER_PIN  2
#define ECHO_PIN     4
#define MAX_DISTANCE 600

NewPingsonar(TRIGGER_PIN, ECHO_PIN, MAX_DISTANCE);
ZumoMotors motors;
long duration, distance;

void setup() {
pinMode(13, OUTPUT);
pinMode(TRIGGER_PIN, OUTPUT);
pinMode(ECHO_PIN, INPUT);
Serial.begin(9600);
}

void loop() {

digitalWrite(TRIGGER_PIN, LOW);
delayMicroseconds(2);

digitalWrite(TRIGGER_PIN, HIGH);
delayMicroseconds(10);

digitalWrite(TRIGGER_PIN, LOW);
duration = pulseIn(ECHO_PIN, HIGH);

  //Calculate the distance (in cm) based on the speed of sound.
distance = duration/58.2;

Serial.println(distance);
motors.setRightSpeed(100);
motors.setLeftSpeed(100);
delay(200);

if(distance <= 20) {

digitalWrite(13, HIGH);   // turn the other way
```

```
motors.setLeftSpeed(-300);
motors.setRightSpeed(100);

delay(200);

}else{
digitalWrite(13, LOW);

motors.setLeftSpeed(100);
motors.setRightSpeed(100);
delay(200);
   }
}
```

Save this program as `ch04_01` and then upload the program into your Arduino board.

Now you can turn on the Pololu Zumo robot. Put the robot in the corner of your room to test whether it can avoid obstacles.

How do we get it to work?

Firstly, we define our Ultrasonic module pins:

```
#define TRIGGER_PIN    2
#define ECHO_PIN       4
#define MAX_DISTANCE 600
NewPingsonar(TRIGGER_PIN, ECHO_PIN, MAX_DISTANCE);
```

We set `TRIGGER_PIN` as the output and `ECHO_PIN` as the input on the `setup()` function:

```
pinMode(TRIGGER_PIN, OUTPUT);
pinMode(ECHO_PIN, INPUT);
```

Then, we spread the signal through `TRIGGER_PIN`. After that, we calculate duration on `ECHO_PIN`.

```
digitalWrite(TRIGGER_PIN, LOW);
delayMicroseconds(2);

digitalWrite(TRIGGER_PIN, HIGH);
delayMicroseconds(10);
digitalWrite(TRIGGER_PIN, LOW);
duration = pulseIn(ECHO_PIN, HIGH);
```

The duration value from the Ultrasonic module is converted to distance by dividing by `58.2`. This value is based on the speed of sound:

```
distance = duration/58.2;
```

If the distance is less than 20 cm, our robot should turn left. You can modify this algorithm on how the robot turns:

```
if(distance <= 20) {
digitalWrite(13, HIGH);   // turn the other way
motors.setLeftSpeed(-300);
motors.setRightSpeed(100);
delay(200);
}else{
digitalWrite(13, LOW);

motors.setLeftSpeed(100);
motors.setRightSpeed(100);
delay(200);
    }
```

Controlling a car robot from a computer

We can control our robot from a computer. This means that we can send commands to the robot to perform an action. In order to send a communication between a computer and robot, we need a communication module on both.

In this section, we will build a communication between the Pololu Zumo robot and a computer. I usually use Bluetooth modules as wireless stacks for communication.

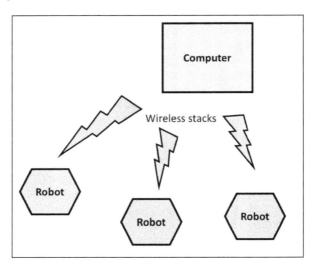

For implementation, I use Bluetooth HC-06. This is a Bluetooth slave, so we can communicate directly through UART protocol. The Bluetooth HC-06 module is cheap, and you can buy it on `banggood.com`, eBay, `dx.com`, and AliExpress.

The Bluetooth HC-06 module has the following four output pins:

- VCC
- GND
- Rx
- Tx

A form of Bluetooth HC-06 module can be seen in the following figure:

To communicate with Bluetooth HC-06, I use the SoftwareSerial library (`https://www.arduino.cc/en/Reference/SoftwareSerial`). This library is supported for the AVR MCU model. If you use an Arduino-based ARM MCU, such as Arduino 101 and Arduino Zero, you can't use the SoftwareSerial library.

For Arduino Leonardo, not all digital pins can be used on a SoftwareSerial library. You can verify it on the SoftwareSerial library website.

In this demo, I will use Arduino Uno R3, which is attached to a Pololu Zumo robot for an Arduino shield.

We define Arduino digital pins 2 and 4 as Rx and Tx so we can connect our Pololu Zumo robot for Arduino to the Bluetooth HC-06 module through a front expansion plate of the Pololu Zumo robot.

The following is a demo wiring:

- Bluetooth HC-06 VCC is connected to a front expansion plate 5V
- Bluetooth HC-06 GND is connected to a front expansion plate GND
- Bluetooth HC-06 Rx is connected to a front expansion plate on pin 4 (Tx)
- Bluetooth HC-06 Tx is connected to a front expansion plate on pin 2 (Rx)

Now we can write a Sketch program to the Pololu Zumo robot for Arduino. Open Arduino IDE and write the following code:

```
#include <ZumoMotors.h>
#include <SoftwareSerial.h>

// D2    >>>  Rx, D4    >>>Tx
SoftwareSerialbluetooth(2, 4); // RX, TX
charval;
ZumoMotors motors;

void setup() {
Serial.begin(9600);
pinMode(13, OUTPUT);
bluetooth.begin(9600);
Serial.println("Bluetooth On..");
}

void loop() {
if(bluetooth.available()){
digitalWrite(13, HIGH);
val = bluetooth.read();

Serial.println(val);
if(val == 'l' ) {
motors.setLeftSpeed(-300);
motors.setRightSpeed(100);
Serial.println("turn left");
    }
if(val == 'r' ) {
motors.setRightSpeed(-300);
```

```
motors.setLeftSpeed(100);
Serial.println("turn right");
    }
if(val == 'f' ) {
motors.setLeftSpeed(100);
motors.setRightSpeed(100);
Serial.println("forward");
    }

digitalWrite(13, LOW);

  }

delay(200);
}
```

Save this program as ch04_02 and upload it to the Arduino board.

On your computer, you should pair the Bluetooth HC-06 with your computer Bluetooth. I use Mac notebook to connect the Bluetooth HC-06. In the Bluetooth settings, you should see Bluetooth HC-06 listed as HC-06.

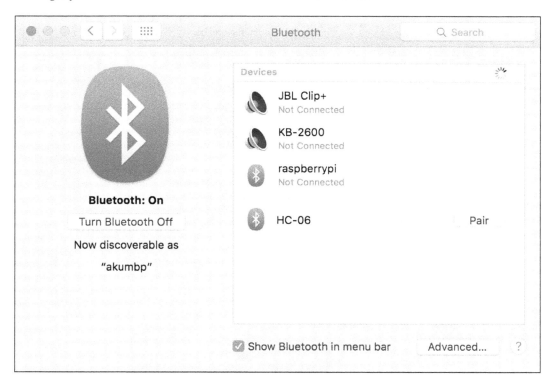

Try to pair it with Bluetooth HC-06. By default, the pair key is 1234.

If you succeed, you should see HC-06 connected to your computer.

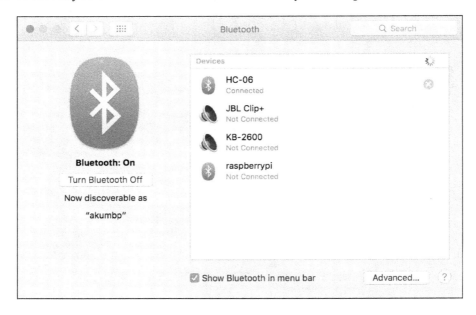

Now you can verify a serial port name for HC-06. You can type the following command on the terminal:

```
$ ls /dev/cu*
```

You should see a serial port name for HC-06. My computer detected it as /dev/cu.HC-06-DevB. We will use this in our program:

```
● ● ●                    ⬆ agusk — -bash — 80×9
agusk$ ls /dev/cu*
/dev/cu.Bluetooth-Incoming-Port /dev/cu.usbmodem1411
/dev/cu.HC-06-DevB
agusk$
```

Now you can write a Python program to access the serial port for HC-06. We will use the pyserial library, https://pypi.python.org/pypi/pyserial, to access the serial port.

If you haven't installed it yet, you can install by typing this command:

```
$ pip install pyserial
```

You may use sudo for installation.

For the next step, we will write a Python program. Write the following code:

```python
import serial

serial_hc06 = '/dev/cu.HC-06-DevB'
counter = 0

print('open ', serial_hc06)
hc06 = serial.Serial(serial_hc06, 9600)

while True:
try:
        # python 3.x
        #c = input('>> ')
```

```
        # python 2.7.x
        c = raw_input('>> ')

if c == 'q':
break

        hc06.write(c)

except (KeyboardInterrupt, SystemExit):
hc06.close()
raise

    print('Exit')
```

You can change the serial_hc06 value for the serial port name from Bluetooth HC-06 module. Save this program to a file called ch04_03.py.

You can run this program using this command:

$ python ch04_03.py

After the code >>appears on the terminal, you can type r, l, and f for turning right, turning left, and moving forward.

To quit the program, you can type q. A sample of the program output can be seen in the following screenshot:

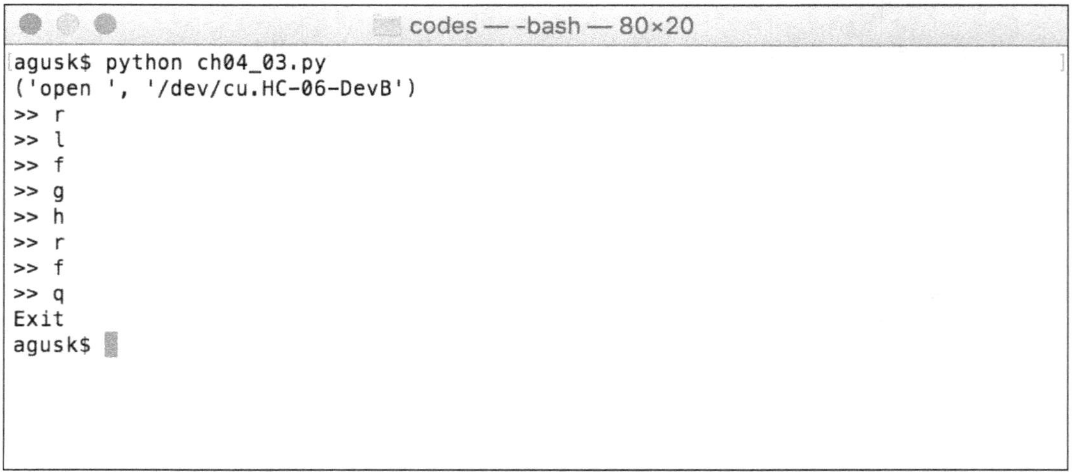

```
● ● ●                    codes — -bash — 80×20
agusk$ python ch04_03.py
('open ', '/dev/cu.HC-06-DevB')
>> r
>> l
>> f
>> g
>> h
>> r
>> f
>> q
Exit
agusk$
```

If the Arduino board is connected to a computer, you can see messages on the Arduino serial port using Serial Monitor. You should see the command character which is sent by the computer.

A sample of the program output on Serial Monitor is shown in the following screenshot:

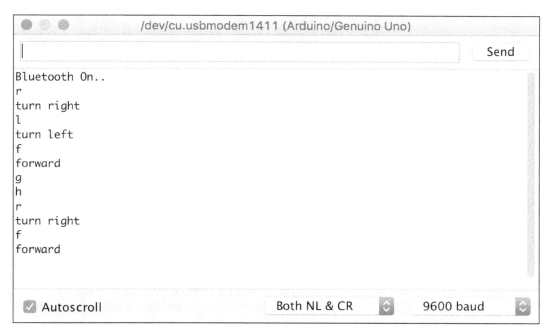

How do we get it to work?

The program is deployed by two devices—Arduino and the computer. The Arduino board, which is attached to the Pololu Zumo robot, receives commands from the computer via Bluetooth.

On the Sketch program, we define the motor and Bluetooth modules:

```
SoftwareSerialbluetooth(2, 4); // RX, TX
charval;
ZumoMotors motors;
```

Then, Pololu Zumo robot will await commands that come from the Bluetooth connection. If the command value is r, the robot will turn right. The command l makes the robot turn left. The command f will make the robot move forward:

```
if(bluetooth.available()){
digitalWrite(13, HIGH);
val = bluetooth.read();

Serial.println(val);
if(val == 'l' ) {
motors.setLeftSpeed(-300);
motors.setRightSpeed(100);
Serial.println("turn left");
    }
if(val == 'r' ) {
motors.setRightSpeed(-300);
motors.setLeftSpeed(100);
Serial.println("turn right");
    }
if(val == 'f' ) {
motors.setLeftSpeed(100);
motors.setRightSpeed(100);
Serial.println("forward");
    }
digitalWrite(13, LOW);
  }
```

On the computer side of the process, we will build a Python program. Basically, it sends data to the Bluetooth connection via the serial port. We use the pyserial library to access the serial port on the computer.

First, we define a serial port named Bluetooth HC-06. You can obtain it after making a connection between HC-06 and the computer's Bluetooth.

```
serial_hc06 = '/dev/cu.HC-06-DevB'
counter = 0
print('open ', serial_hc06)
hc06 = serial.Serial(serial_hc06, 9600)
```

After the serial port is opened, the computer awaits character input from the user. Once a character is obtained, a program will pass it to the serial port:

```
# python 3.x
#c = input('>> ')

# python 2.7.x
c = raw_input('>> ')
```

The program will exit if the user types the character q.

Working with a GPS module for navigation

GPS is module that receives a certain location from a satellite. GPS is a good method for finding a location when outdoors. Several GPS satellites can be used in the GPS module.

In this section, we will try to access a location from a GPS module. Location information obtained from the satellite will be sent to a computer through Bluetooth.

We will use the U-blox NEO-6M Module to retrieve the location from the satellite. We will use the same Bluetooth module, HC-06, in this demo. A computer will listen to the GPS data from a robot. The GPS data that are sent are latitude and longitude coordinates.

I obtained a U-blox NEO-6M from dx.com (http://www.dx.com/p/gps-module-w-ceramic-passive-antenna-for-raspberry-pi-arduino-red-384916). This module is cheap, and you can buy it on Banggood, eBay and AliExpress.

A form of U-blox NEO-6M module is shown in the following figure:

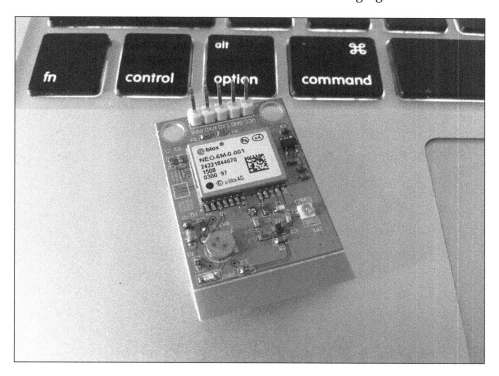

U-blox NEO-6M Module provides TTL output so we can access the data easily. GPS data from this module is raw data, so we need a GPS data parser. To encode GPS data, we will use the TinyGPS library, found at `https://github.com/mikalhart/TinyGPS`. Please download TinyGPS and put it in the Arduino library.

The next step is to build a demo wiring. You can see the wiring on the following figure:

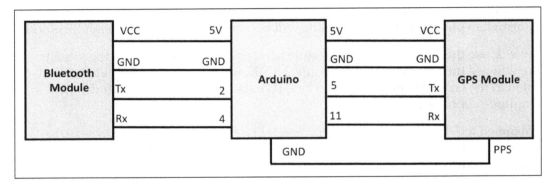

This wiring picture is summarized as follows:

- **Bluetooth Module**: This has the following connections:
    - Bluetooth VCC is connected to Arduino 5V
    - Bluetooth GND is connected to Arduino GND
    - Bluetooth Tx is connected to Arduino pin 2
    - Bluetooth Rx is connected to Arduino pin 4
- **GPS Module**: This has the following connections:
    - GPS VCC is connected to Arduino 5V
    - Bluetooth GND is connected to Arduino GND
    - Bluetooth Tx is connected to Arduino pin 5
    - Bluetooth Rx is connected to Arduino pin 11
    - Bluetooth PPS is connected to Arduino GND

The next step is to write the program on Arduino. Open Arduino IDE and write the following Sketch program:

```
#include <SoftwareSerial.h>
#include <TinyGPS.h>

// D2    >>>  Rx, D4    >>>Tx
SoftwareSerialbluetooth(2, 4); // RX, TX

// D5    >>>  Rx, D11   >>>Tx
SoftwareSerialgps(5, 11);  // RX, TX
charval;
TinyGPSgps_mod;

void setup() {
Serial.begin(9600);
pinMode(13, OUTPUT);
bluetooth.begin(9600);
Serial.println("Bluetooth On..");
gps.begin(9600);
Serial.println("GPS On..");
}

void loop() {
boolnewData = false;
unsigned long chars;
unsigned short sentences, failed;

  // read GPS position every 3 seconds
for (unsigned long start = millis(); millis() - start < 3000;) {
while (gps.available()){
char c = gps.read();
      //Serial.println(c);
if (gps_mod.encode(c))
newData = true;
    }
  }

if (newData) {
float flat, flon;
unsigned long age;

digitalWrite(13, HIGH);
gps_mod.f_get_position(&flat, &flon, &age);
```

```
print_data("LAT=");
print_num_data(flat == TinyGPS::GPS_INVALID_F_ANGLE ? 0.0 : flat, 6);
print_data(" LON=");
print_num_data(flon == TinyGPS::GPS_INVALID_F_ANGLE ? 0.0 : flon, 6);
print_data(" SAT=");
print_num_data(gps_mod.satellites() == TinyGPS::GPS_INVALID_SATELLITES
? 0 : gps_mod.satellites());
print_data(" PREC=");
print_num_data(gps_mod.hdop() == TinyGPS::GPS_INVALID_HDOP ? 0 : gps_
mod.hdop());

break_line();
digitalWrite(13, LOW);
   }
}

voidprint_data(char msg[30]) {
Serial.print(msg);
bluetooth.print(msg);
}
voidprint_num_data(float msg,int n) {
Serial.print(msg, n);
bluetooth.print(msg, n);
}
voidprint_num_data(intmsg) {
Serial.print(msg);
bluetooth.print(msg);
}
voidbreak_line() {
Serial.println("");
bluetooth.println("");
}
```

Save this program as ch04_04.

Then, you can compile and upload the program onto the Arduino board. After that, attach the Arduino board to the Pololu Zumo robot for Arduino.

On the computer, you should establish a Bluetooth connection between HC-06 and the computer's Bluetooth. You already did this in the previous section. In this case, my HC-06 is recognized as /dev/cu.HC-06-DevB on my Mac machine.

Now we will write a Python program to listen to incoming messages, namely GPS data from the Arduino board.

Write the following program:

```
import serial
import sys

serial_hc06 = '/dev/cu.HC-06-DevB'
counter = 0

print('open ', serial_hc06)
hc06 = serial.Serial(serial_hc06, 9600)
print('read data from gps')
while True:
try:
        c = hc06.read(1)
if c != '':
sys.stdout.write(c)
sys.stdout.flush()

except (KeyboardInterrupt, SystemExit):
hc06.close()
raise

print('Exit')
```

Please change the `serial_hc06` value with your serial port name of HC-06 paired with Bluetooth.

When this is done, save this program to a file under the name of `ch04_05.py`.

To test everything out, you can run the program by typing this command:

`$ python ch04_05.py`

Make sure that the Arduino board is already turned on.

If everything is successfully set up, you should be able to obtain the GPS data from Arduino through Bluetooth. A sample of the program output is shown in the following screenshot:

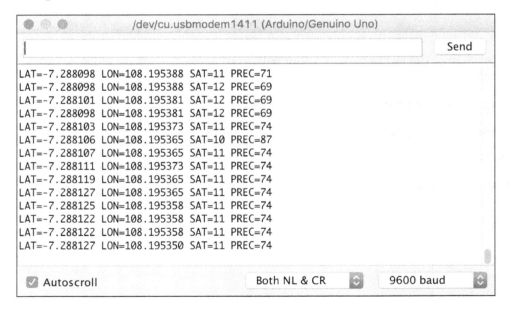

```
agusk$ python ch04_05.py
('open ', '/dev/cu.HC-06-DevB')
read data from gps
LAT=-7.288106 LON=108.195365 SAT=10 PREC=87
LAT=-7.288107 LON=108.195365 SAT=11 PREC=74
LAT=-7.288111 LON=108.195373 SAT=11 PREC=74
LAT=-7.288119 LON=108.195365 SAT=11 PREC=74
LAT=-7.288127 LON=108.195365 SAT=11 PREC=74
LAT=-7.288125 LON=108.195358 SAT=11 PREC=74
LAT=-7.288122 LON=108.195358 SAT=11 PREC=74
LAT=-7.288122 LON=108.195358 SAT=11 PREC=74
```

If your Arduino is connected to the computer via USB, you can see the messages using the Serial Monitor tool.

A sample of the program output on the Serial Monitor tool can be seen in the following screenshot:

```
LAT=-7.288098 LON=108.195388 SAT=11 PREC=71
LAT=-7.288098 LON=108.195388 SAT=12 PREC=69
LAT=-7.288101 LON=108.195381 SAT=12 PREC=69
LAT=-7.288098 LON=108.195381 SAT=12 PREC=69
LAT=-7.288103 LON=108.195373 SAT=11 PREC=74
LAT=-7.288106 LON=108.195365 SAT=10 PREC=87
LAT=-7.288107 LON=108.195365 SAT=11 PREC=74
LAT=-7.288111 LON=108.195373 SAT=11 PREC=74
LAT=-7.288119 LON=108.195365 SAT=11 PREC=74
LAT=-7.288127 LON=108.195365 SAT=11 PREC=74
LAT=-7.288125 LON=108.195358 SAT=11 PREC=74
LAT=-7.288122 LON=108.195358 SAT=11 PREC=74
LAT=-7.288122 LON=108.195358 SAT=11 PREC=74
LAT=-7.288127 LON=108.195350 SAT=11 PREC=74
```

How do we get this to work?

This program works in the same way as the previous Bluetooth demo. In this demo, however, we add an additional module to the Pololu Zumo robot, that is, the GPS module. To parse the GPS data, which is obtained from satellite, we use the TinyGPS library. Firstly, we define the GPS module on digital pins 5 and 11 from the Pololu Zumo robot.

```
// D5    >>>  Rx, D11    >>>Tx
SoftwareSerialgps(5, 11);  // RX, TX
charval;
TinyGPSgps_mod;
```

On the `setup()` function, we initialize Bluetooth and the GPS modules, including the Serial object.

```
void setup() {
Serial.begin(9600);
pinMode(13, OUTPUT);
bluetooth.begin(9600);
Serial.println("Bluetooth On..");
gps.begin(9600);
Serial.println("GPS On.."); }
```

Every three seconds, we will try to read the data on the GPS module. It happens on the `loop()` function.

```
for (unsigned long start = millis(); millis() - start < 3000;) {
while (gps.available()){
char c = gps.read();
    //Serial.println(c);
    if (gps_mod.encode(c))  newData = true;
  }
}
```

If the received data is valid for the GPS data, we will parse this data using the TinyGPS library. We will send this data to the Bluetooth module and Arduino serial port.

```
if (newData) {
float flat, flon;
unsigned long age;

digitalWrite(13, HIGH);
gps_mod.f_get_position(&flat, &flon, &age);
```

```
print_data("LAT=");
print_num_data(flat == TinyGPS::GPS_INVALID_F_ANGLE ? 0.0 : flat, 6);
print_data(" LON=");
print_num_data(flon == TinyGPS::GPS_INVALID_F_ANGLE ? 0.0 : flon, 6);
print_data(" SAT=");
print_num_data(gps_mod.satellites() == TinyGPS::GPS_INVALID_SATELLITES
? 0 : gps_mod.satellites());
print_data(" PREC=");
print_num_data(gps_mod.hdop() == TinyGPS::GPS_INVALID_HDOP ? 0 :
  gps_mod.hdop());
break_line();
digitalWrite(13, LOW);     }
```

On the computer side, we will just open the serial port for HC-06 paired with Bluetooth.

```
serial_hc06 = '/dev/cu.HC-06-DevB'
counter = 0

print('open ', serial_hc06)
hc06 = serial.Serial(serial_hc06, 9600)
```

Once it has opened, the program will wait for the incoming message from Bluetooth. Once it has received the data, the program prints it into the Terminal.

```
c = hc06.read(1)
if c != '':
sys.stdout.write(c)
sys.stdout.flush()
```

Introducing map engine platforms

To visualize our GPS data into concepts such as latitude and longitude, we can use a map. By putting latitude and longitude values on a map, we can see the exact location of the entity in question.

Basically, you can use your own map to visualize our GPS data. In this section, we will learn the common map engine platform, Google Maps API. This library provides many options for our programming model to visualize GPS data on a map. For further information about Google Maps API, you can visit the official website at https://developers.google.com/maps.

For our demo, we will use Google Maps API on our Python program. I use the Flask library as a web framework. Please find the Flask library at http://flask.pocoo. org.

To install the Flash library on your computer or Raspberry Pi, you can get it via pip:

```
$ pip install Flask
```

You may need to be of administrator level in order to install it. If so, you can use sudo on your command. For a Windows platform, you can call Command Prompts that run for an administrator level user.

For our demo, we will create a simple Flask app, gpsapp.py. Type the following commands:

```
$ mkdirgps_web
```

```
$ cdgps_web
```

```
$ nano gspapp.py
```

Now you can write the following program on the gpsapp.py file:

```
from flask import Flask
from flask import render_template
from flask import jsonify

app = Flask(__name__)


@app.route('/hello')
defhello_world():
return 'Hello, World!'
```

Save this program. To run this program, you can use the following commands:

```
$ export FLASK_APP=gpsapp.py
```

```
$ python -m flask run
```

By default, the program runs on port 5000, so you open your browser and navigate to http://localhost:5000/hello. You should see **Hello, World!** on your browser.

A sample of program output on the browser can be seen in the following screenshot:

On the Terminal on which your program runs, you should see request messages from the browser. A sample of the program output on the Terminal is shown in the following screenshot:

```
● ● ●                gps_web — Python -m flask run — 80×20
agusk$ python3 -m flask run
 * Serving Flask app "gpsapp"
 * Running on http://127.0.0.1:5000/ (Press CTRL+C to quit)
127.0.0.1 - - [06/Jul/2016 20:50:41] "GET /tracking HTTP/1.1" 200 -
127.0.0.1 - - [06/Jul/2016 20:50:42] "GET / HTTP/1.1" 200 -
127.0.0.1 - - [06/Jul/2016 20:50:42] "GET /hello HTTP/1.1" 200 -
127.0.0.1 - - [06/Jul/2016 20:50:43] "GET /hello HTTP/1.1" 200 -
```

How do we get it to work?

In our program, we will define a route `/hello` on the `gpsapp.py` file and send a response `Hello World!` to the requester:

```
@app.route('/hello')
defhello_world():
return 'Hello, World!'
```

We will continue to integrate our program, `gpsapp.py`, with Google Maps.

Create a template folder inside our program folder. Then, create a file, `index.html`. Write the following scripts on the `index.html` file:

```
<!doctype html>
<html lang="en">
<head>
<title>Google Maps Demo</title>
<meta name="viewport" content="initial-scale=1.0, user-scalable=no" />
<scriptsrc="http://maps.google.com/maps/api/js?sensor=false"></script>
<script>
var map;
function initialize() {
varmyCenter = new google.maps.LatLng(52.524343, 13.412751);
map = new google.maps.Map(document.getElementById('map'), {
zoom: 5,
center: myCenter,
mapTypeId: google.maps.MapTypeId.ROADMAP
        });
var marker=new google.maps.Marker({
position:myCenter
        });
marker.setMap(map);
    }
</script>
<style>
body {font-family: sans-serif}
        #map {width: 640px; height: 480px}
</style>
</head>
<body onload='initialize()'>
<div id=map></div>
</body>
</html>
```

These scripts will load Google Maps API via JavaScript. Furthermore, we will create a google.maps.Map object. We will pass latitude and longitude, for instance, 52.524343,13.412751. You can change it if you want.

We will also define a marker using the google.maps.Marker object on our latitude and longitude points.

Now we must modify the gpsapp.py file to add additional routing. The following is completed code for the gpsapp.py file.

```
from flask import Flask
from flask import render_template
from flask import jsonify

app = Flask(__name__)


@app.route('/hello')
defhello_world():
return 'Hello, World!'


@app.route('/')
def index(name=None):
returnrender_template('index.html', name=name)
```

Now you can run the gpsapp.py file again on the Terminal. After that, you can open a browser and navigate to http://localhost:5000/. Make sure the computer running this browser is already connected to the Internet because the program index.html requires Google Maps API.

A sample of the program output on the browser can be seen in the following screenshot:

Building a car-based GPS

In the previous section, we learned how to access Google Maps API on a Python program using the Flask library. Now we can combine our previous work about reading GPS on the Pololu Zumo robot.

After the program reads the GPS data on Arduino, we can send the GPS data to our web server (Flask framework).

Firstly, we modify gpsapp.py to read the GPS data. You can read it directly from the GPS module or via the middleware app on the computer.

We will create a new routing /gps which is implemented on the get_gps_data() function. With this function, we will set the value "hardcoded". Basically, you should get lat_val and long_val from the GPS module. The get_gps_data() function returns a JSON value. This makes our program, gspapp.py, work as a RESTful server.

The following is a completed program on the gpsapp.py file:

```python
from flask import Flask
from flask import render_template
from flask import jsonify

app = Flask(__name__)


@app.route('/hello')
defhello_world():
return 'Hello, World!'


@app.route('/')
def index(name=None):
returnrender_template('index.html', name=name)


@app.route('/tracking')
def tracking(name=None):
returnrender_template('tracking.html', name=name)


@app.route('/gps', methods=['GET'])
defget_gps_data():

    # get data from robot via wireless module such as GSM, WiFi,
Bluetooth
lat_val = 52.524343
long_val = 13.412751

returnjsonify(lat=lat_val, long=long_val)
```

Save this program.

The next step is to create an HTML file. Create a file called tracking.html. Put this file in the templates folder.

With `tracking.html`, we will do the same thing as we did with `index.html`, but latitude and longitude values are obtained from the server. We will use jQuery to retrieve data from the server. We will use a timer by calling `setInterval()` to call the RESTful server every 5 seconds:

```html
<!doctype html>
<html lang="en">
<head>
<title>Robot Tracking Demo</title>
<meta name="viewport" content="initial-scale=1.0, user-scalable=no" />
<script src="https://ajax.googleapis.com/ajax/libs/jquery/1.12.4/
jquery.min.js"></script>
<scriptsrc="http://maps.google.com/maps/api/js?sensor=false"></script>
<style>
body {font-family: sans-serif}
        #map {width: 640px; height: 480px}
</style>
</head>
<body>
<div id=map></div>

<script>
var map;
varisLoading = false;

functionload_maps(lat,long) {
varmyCenter = new google.maps.LatLng(lat, long);
map = new google.maps.Map(document.getElementById('map'), {
zoom: 5,
center: myCenter,
mapTypeId: google.maps.MapTypeId.ROADMAP
            });
var marker=new google.maps.Marker({
position:myCenter
            });
marker.setMap(map);
isLoading = false;
        }


setInterval(function(){
if(!isLoading) {
```

```
        isLoading = true;
                    $.getJSON("/gps", function(result){
load_maps(result.lat, result.long);
                    });


            }
        }, 5000);
</script>
</body>
</html>
```

Save this program.

Now you can run this program and navigate to `http://localhost:5000/tracking`. You should see a map, complete with annotations and markings. This page will refresh every 5 seconds.

You already know how to track a robot using a browser. Can you control your robot from a website? You can try this as an exercise.

Making your own autonomous car

All materials to build an autonomous car have been provided. Now you can own an autonomous car based on your requirements. You can make an autonomous ,mobile machine tailored to a specific task, for instance, a vacuum cleaner robot. You can use an Ultrasonic module to detect obstacles.

In my opinion, the big issue in making a vacuum cleaner robot is the cleaning path algorithm—how the robot visits all areas. It happens because the robot doesn't have a map. You could use a microSD card module to store every visited area. With a semi-autonomous robot, we can use middleware to guide the robot about a cleaning path.

Consider the example of Roomba from iRobot `http://www.irobot.com/For-the-Home/Vacuuming/Roomba.aspx`. I found out that the Roomba robot uses the cleaning path algorithm shown in the following figure:

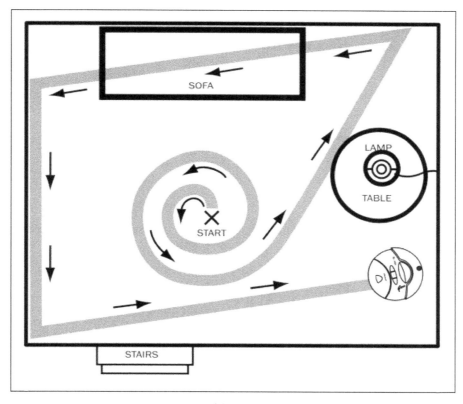

Source: https://www.irobot.com/

Read these papers (4,5,6) to get an idea of how to build a vacuum cleaner robot.

By integrating sensor and actuator devices, you can expand your imagination to build an autonomous robot.

Summary

In this chapter, we learned some basic techniques in building an autonomous robot. We also explored several robot platforms on which to build your own robot project. We took one of the robot platforms, the Pololu Zumo robot for Arduino, for our exercise. We integrated the robot with navigation module to build a navigated robot. For the last topic, we tracked our robot with the map engine Google Maps API.

In the next chapter, we will learn how to integrate voice technology into your smart IoT projects.

References

The following is a list of recommend papers, books, and websites from which you can learn more about the topics in this chapter:

1. Meystel, A.: *Intelligent Control: A Sketch of the Theory, 1. Intelligent and Robotic Systems*, Vol. 2, 1989, pp. 97-107.

2. *Autonomous Robotic Systems. Lecture Notes in Control and Information Sciences*, Springer, 1998.

3. *Advances in Intelligent Autonomous System. International Series on MICROPROCESSOR-BASED AND INTELLIGENT SYSTEMS ENGINEERING*, Vol. 18, Springer Science + Business Media Dordrecht, 1999.

4. K. M. Hasan, Abdullah-Al-Nahid and K. J. Reza, *Path planning algorithm development for autonomous vacuum cleaner robots*, **Informatics, Electronics & Vision (ICIEV)**, 2014 International Conference on, Dhaka, 2014, pp. 1–6.

5. Sewan Kim, *Autonomous cleaning robot: Roboking system integration and overview*, Robotics and Automation, 2004. Proceedings, ICRA '04.2004 IEEE International Conference on, 2004, pp. 4437-41 Vol. 5.

6. Ryo Kurazume, Shigeo Hirose, *Development of a Cleaning Robot System with Cooperative Positioning System* in Autonomous Robots (2000) Volume 9, Issue: 3, Springer, pp. 237–46.

7. Flask, http://flask.pocoo.org.

8. Google Maps API, https://developers.google.com/maps.

5

Building Voice Technology on IoT Projects

In this chapter, we explore how to make your IoT board speak something. Various sound and speech modules will be explored as project journey.

We explore the following topics

- Introduce a speech technology
- Introduce sound sensor and actuator
- Introduce pattern recognition for speech technology
- Review speech and sound modules
- Build your own voice commands for IoT projects
- Make your IoT board speak
- Make Raspberry Pi speak

Introduce a speech technology

Speech is the primary means of communication among people. A speech technology is a technology which is built by speech recognition research. A machine such as a computer can understand what human said even the machine can recognize each speech model so the machine can differentiate each human's speech.

A speech technology covers speech-to-text and text-to-speech topics. Some researchers already define several speech model for some languages, for instance, English, German, China, French.

A general of speech research topics can be seen in the following figure:

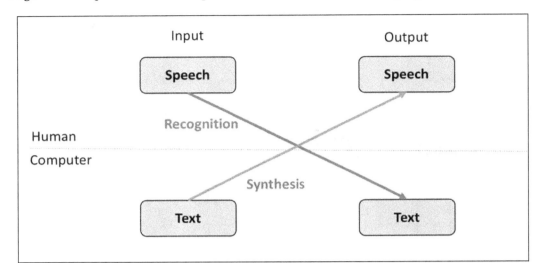

To convert speech to text, we should understand about speech recognition. Otherwise, if we want to generate speech sounds from text, we should learn about speech synthesis. This book doesn't cover about speech recognition and speech synthesis in heavy mathematics and statistics approach. I recommend you read textbook related to those topics.

In this chapter, we will learn how to work sound and speech processing on IoT platform environment.

Introduce sound sensors and actuators

Sound sources can come from human, animal, car, and so on . To process sound data, we should capture the sound source from physical to digital form. This happens if we use sensor devices which capture the physical sound source. A simple sound sensor is microphone. This sensor can record any source via microphone.

We use a microphone module which is connected to your IoT board, for instance, Arduino and Raspberry Pi. One of them is Electret Microphone Breakout, https://www.sparkfun.com/products/12758. This is a breakout module which exposes three pin outs: **AUD, GND,** and **VCC.** You can see it in the following figure.

Furthermore, we can generate sound using an actuator. A simple sound actuator is passive buzzer. This component can generate simple sounds with limited frequency. You can generate sound by sending on signal pin through analog output or **PWM** pin. Some manufacturers also provide a breakout module for buzzer. Buzzer actuator form is shown in the following figure.

Buzzer usually is passive actuator. If you want to work with active sound actuator, you can use a speaker. This component is easy to find on your local or online store. I also found it on Sparkfun, `https://www.sparkfun.com/products/11089` which you can see it in the following figure.

To get experiences how to work sound sensor/actuator, we build a demo to capture sound source by getting sound intensity.

In this demo, I show how to detect a sound intensity level using sound sensor, an Electret microphone. The sound source can come from sounds of voice, claps, door knocks or any sounds loud enough to be picked up by a sensor device. The output of sensor device is analog value so MCU should convert it via a microcontroller's analog-to-digital converter.

The following is a list of peripheral for our demo.

- Arduino board
- Resistor 330 Ohm
- Electret Microphone Breakout, `https://www.sparkfun.com/products/12758`
- 10 Segment LED Bar Graph - Red, `https://www.sparkfun.com/products/9935`. You can use any color for LED bar

You can also use Adafruit Electret Microphone Breakout to be attached into Arduino board. You can review it on `https://www.adafruit.com/product/1063`.

To build our demo, you wire those components as follows

- Connect Electret Microphone **AUD** pin to Arduino **A0** pin
- Connect Electret Microphone **GND** pin to Arduino **GND** pin

- Connect Electret Microphone **VCC** pin to Arduino **3.3V** pin
- Connect 10 Segment LED Bar Graph pins to Arduino digital pins: **3**, **4**, **5**, **6**, **7**, **8**, **9**, **10**, **11**, **12** which already connected to resistor 330 Ohm

You can see the final wiring of our demo in the following figure:

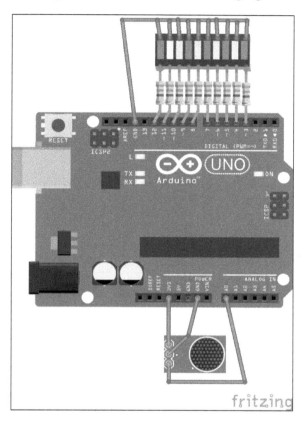

10 segment led bar graph module is used to represent of sound intensity level. In Arduino we can use `analogRead()` to read analog input from external sensor. Output of `analogRead()` returns value `0 - 1023`.

Total output in voltage is 3.3V because we connect Electret Microphone Breakout with 3.3V on VCC. From this situation, we can set *3.3/10 = 0.33* voltage for each segment led bar. The first segment led bar is connected to Arduino digital pin **3**.

Now we can implement to build our sketch program to read sound intensity and then convert measurement value into 10 segment led bar graph.

To obtain a sound intensity, we try to read sound input from analog input pin. We read it during a certain time, called sample window time, for instance, 250 ms. During that time, we should get the peak value or maximum value of analog input. The peak value will be set as sound intensity value.

Let's start to implement our program. Open Arduino IDE and write the following sketch program.

```
// Sample window width in mS (250 mS = 4Hz)
const int sampleWindow = 250;
unsigned int sound;
int led = 13;

void setup()
{
    Serial.begin(9600);
    pinMode(led, OUTPUT);

    pinMode(3, OUTPUT);
    pinMode(4, OUTPUT);
    pinMode(5, OUTPUT);
    pinMode(6, OUTPUT);
    pinMode(7, OUTPUT);
    pinMode(8, OUTPUT);
    pinMode(9, OUTPUT);
    pinMode(10, OUTPUT);
    pinMode(11, OUTPUT);
    pinMode(12, OUTPUT);
}

void loop()
{
  unsigned long start= millis();
  unsigned int peakToPeak = 0;

  unsigned int signalMax = 0;
  unsigned int signalMin = 1024;

  // collect data for 250 milliseconds
  while (millis() - start < sampleWindow)
  {
    sound = analogRead(0);
    if (sound < 1024)
    {
```

```
      if (sound > signalMax)
      {
        signalMax = sound;
      }
      else if (sound < signalMin)
      {
        signalMin = sound;
      }
    }
  }
  peakToPeak = signalMax - signalMin;
  double volts = (peakToPeak * 3.3) / 1024;

  Serial.println(volts);
  display_bar_led(volts);
}

void display_bar_led(double volts)
{
  display_bar_led_off();

  int index = round(volts/0.33);
  switch(index){
    case 1:
      digitalWrite(3, HIGH);
      break;
    case 2:
      digitalWrite(3, HIGH);
      digitalWrite(3, HIGH);
      break;
    case 3:
      digitalWrite(3, HIGH);
      digitalWrite(4, HIGH);
      digitalWrite(5, HIGH);
      break;
    case 4:
      digitalWrite(3, HIGH);
      digitalWrite(4, HIGH);
      digitalWrite(5, HIGH);
      digitalWrite(6, HIGH);
      break;
    case 5:
      digitalWrite(3, HIGH);
      digitalWrite(4, HIGH);
```

```
    digitalWrite(5, HIGH);
    digitalWrite(6, HIGH);
    digitalWrite(7, HIGH);
    break;
  case 6:
    digitalWrite(3, HIGH);
    digitalWrite(4, HIGH);
    digitalWrite(5, HIGH);
    digitalWrite(6, HIGH);
    digitalWrite(7, HIGH);
    digitalWrite(8, HIGH);
    break;
  case 7:
    digitalWrite(3, HIGH);
    digitalWrite(4, HIGH);
    digitalWrite(5, HIGH);
    digitalWrite(6, HIGH);
    digitalWrite(7, HIGH);
    digitalWrite(8, HIGH);
    digitalWrite(9, HIGH);
    break;
  case 8:
    digitalWrite(3, HIGH);
    digitalWrite(4, HIGH);
    digitalWrite(5, HIGH);
    digitalWrite(6, HIGH);
    digitalWrite(7, HIGH);
    digitalWrite(8, HIGH);
    digitalWrite(9, HIGH);
    digitalWrite(10, HIGH);
    break;
  case 9:
    digitalWrite(3, HIGH);
    digitalWrite(4, HIGH);
    digitalWrite(5, HIGH);
    digitalWrite(6, HIGH);
    digitalWrite(7, HIGH);
    digitalWrite(8, HIGH);
    digitalWrite(9, HIGH);
```

```
      digitalWrite(10, HIGH);
      digitalWrite(11, HIGH);
      break;
    case 10:
      digitalWrite(3, HIGH);
      digitalWrite(4, HIGH);
      digitalWrite(5, HIGH);
      digitalWrite(6, HIGH);
      digitalWrite(7, HIGH);
      digitalWrite(8, HIGH);
      digitalWrite(9, HIGH);
      digitalWrite(10, HIGH);
      digitalWrite(11, HIGH);
      digitalWrite(12, HIGH);
      break;
  }

}

void display_bar_led_off()
{
  digitalWrite(3, LOW);
  digitalWrite(4, LOW);
  digitalWrite(5, LOW);
  digitalWrite(6, LOW);
  digitalWrite(7, LOW);
  digitalWrite(8, LOW);
  digitalWrite(9, LOW);
  digitalWrite(10, LOW);
  digitalWrite(11, LOW);
  digitalWrite(12, LOW);
}
```

Save this sketch program as ch05_01.

Compile and deploy this program into Arduino board.

After deployed the program, you can open **Serial Plotter** tool. You can find this tool from **Arduino menu Tools - | Serial Plotter**. Set the baud rate as 9600 baud on the Serial Plotter tool.

Try to make noise on a sound sensor device. You can see changing values on graphs from Serial Plotter tool. A sample of Serial Plotter can be seen in the following figure:

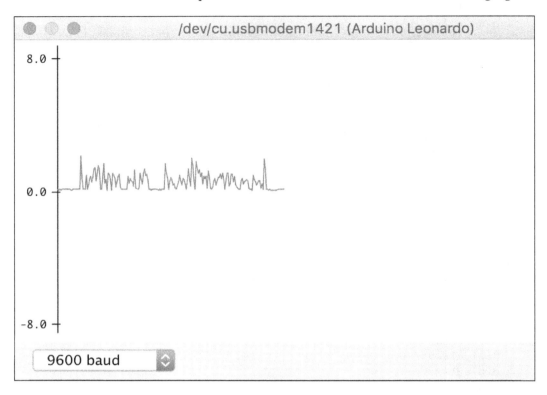

How to work?

The idea to obtain a sound intensity is easy. We get a value among sound signal peaks. Firstly, we define a sample width, for instance, 250 ms for 4Hz.

```
// Sample window width in mS (250 mS = 4Hz)
const int sampleWindow = 250;
unsigned int sound;

int led = 13;
```

On the setup() function, we initialize serial port and our 10 segment led bar graph.

```
void setup()
{
    Serial.begin(9600);
    pinMode(led, OUTPUT);
```

```
    pinMode(3, OUTPUT);
    pinMode(4, OUTPUT);
    pinMode(5, OUTPUT);
    pinMode(6, OUTPUT);
    pinMode(7, OUTPUT);
    pinMode(8, OUTPUT);
    pinMode(9, OUTPUT);
    pinMode(10, OUTPUT);
    pinMode(11, OUTPUT);
    pinMode(12, OUTPUT);


}
```

On the `loop()` function, we perform to calculate a sound intensity related to a sample width. After obtained a peak-to-peak value, we convert it into voltage form.

```
unsigned long start= millis();
unsigned int peakToPeak = 0;

unsigned int signalMax = 0;
unsigned int signalMin = 1024;

// collect data for 250 milliseconds
while (millis() - start < sampleWindow)
{
  sound = analogRead(0);
  if (sound < 1024)
  {
    if (sound > signalMax)
    {
     signalMax = sound;
    }
    else if (sound < signalMin)
    {
      signalMin = sound;
    }
  }
}
peakToPeak = signalMax - signalMin;

double volts = (peakToPeak * 3.3) / 1024;
```

Then, we show a sound intensity in volt form in serial port and 10 segment led by calling `display_bar_led()`.

```
Serial.println(volts);

display_bar_led(volts);
```

Inside the `display_bar_led()` function, we turn off all LEDs on 10 segment led bar graph by calling `display_bar_led_off()` which sends LOW on all LEDs using `digitalWrite()`. After that, we calculate a range value from volts. This value will be converted as total showing LEDs.

```
display_bar_led_off();
int index = round(volts/0.33);
```

Introduce pattern recognition for speech technology

Pattern recognition is one of topic in machine learning and as baseline for speech recognition. In general, we can construct speech recognition system in the following figure:

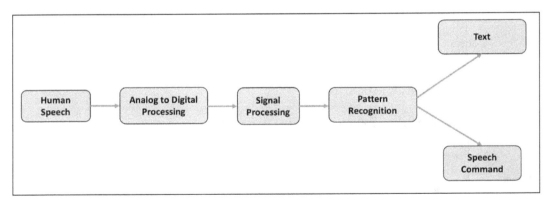

From human speech, we should convert it into digital form, called discrete data. Some signal processing methods are applied to handle pre-processing such as removing noise from data.

Now in pattern recognition we do perform speech recognition method. Researchers did some approaches such as computing using **Hidden Markov Model (HMM)** to identity sound related to word. Performing feature extraction in speech digital data is a part of pattern recognition activities. The output will be used as input in pattern recognition input.

The output of pattern recognition can be applied as `Speech-to-Text` and `Speech` command on our IoT projects.

Reviewing speech and sound modules for IoT devices

In this section, we review various speech and sound modules which can be integrated into our MCU board. There are a lot of modules related to speech and sound processing. Each module has unique features which fits with your works.

One of speech and sound modules is **EasyVR 3 & EasyVR Shield 3** from VeeaR. You can review this module on `http://www.veear.eu/introducing-easyvr-3-easyvr-shield-3/`. Several languages already have been supported such as English (US), Italian, German, French, Spanish, and Japanese.

You can see EasyVR 3 module in the following figure:

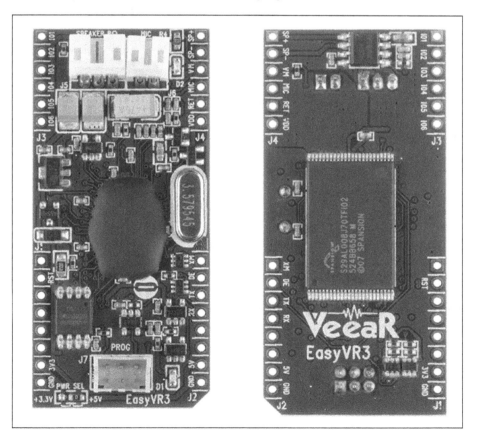

EasyVR 3 board also is available as a shield for Arduino. If you buy an EasyVR Shield 3, you will obtain EasyVR board and its Arduino shield. You can see the form of EasyVR Shield 3 on the following figure:

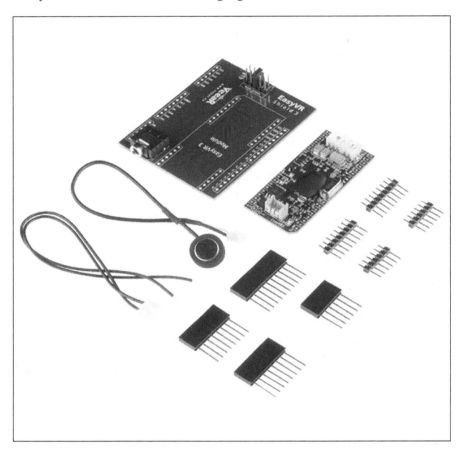

The second module is Emic 2. It was designed by Parallax in conjunction with Grand Idea Studio, http:// www.grandideastudio.com/, to make voice synthesis a total no-brainer. You can send texts to the module to generate human speech through serial protocol. This module is useful if you want to make boards speak. Further information about this module, you can visit and buy this module on https://www. parallax.com/product/30016. The following is a form of Emic-2 module:

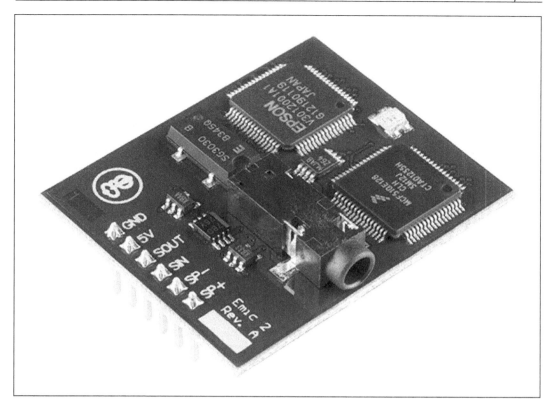

Build your own voice commands for IoT projects

It's nice if you can turn on/off lamps via voice commands. Yes, in this section, we will build a simple project to build voice commands on Arduino. We use EasyVR 3 shield for Arduino.

Our scenario is to build voice commands on Arduino to turn on/off a LED. You can change LED with a relay module and lamp. For development environment, I use Windows OS to implement this demo. Some EasyVR tools run only on Windows platform. For testing, I use Arduino Uno R3 board.

Let's start!

Setting up EasyVR shield 3

Before you using EasyVR shield 3 into your program, you should prepare to install several software and libraries.

Firstly, download EasyVR library for Arduino. You can download it on `https://github.com/RoboTech-srl/EasyVR-Arduino/releases`. Extract the file and put it on your Arduino library folder. You also can do it by clicking menu **Sketch | Include Library | Add .ZIP Library**. Select EasyVR library ZIP file.

The next step is to install EasyVR Commander tools on `http://www.veear.eu/downloads/`. Download and install by following the instruction. After installed, you should get several tools. We will use these tools for configuring EasyVR module. I'll explain them on the next section.

Soldering EasyVR shield 3 breakout and attach into your Arduino board. In this case, I used Arduino Uno R3.

The layout of EasyVR shield 3 can be seen in the following figure:

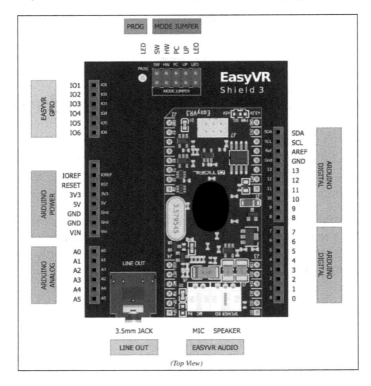

(Top View)

To work with EasyVR module, we set **MODE JUMPER** to **PC**. Then, connect your Arduino with EasyVR shield into your computer through USB.

Your computer should detect Arduino board. You can see it on **Device Manager** in Windows platform which shows in **Ports (COM & LPT)**.

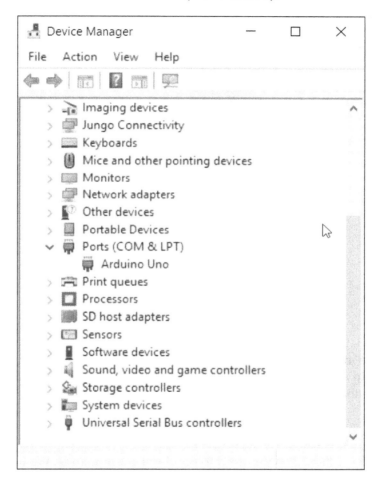

Now you can open EasyVR Commander tool. Select serial port where Arduino is connected. Select a serial port for Arduino with EasyVR module and connect it. A sample of EasyVR Commander tool already connected with EasyVR module, shown in the following figure:

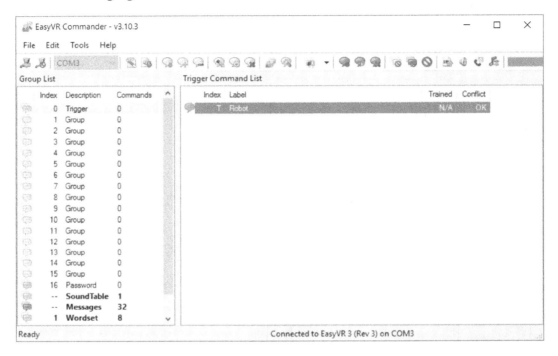

You should see index 0... 16. `Trigger` and `Password` are reserved group index. I explain how to use EasyVR Commander tool in order to Arduino understand your voice commands.

Building voice commands

The thing that you should configure is to build voice commands. We use EasyVR Commander tool. We will build the following voice command models:

- `ARDUINO` is used to start our program
- `MYPASS` is used for password
- `LAMP_ON` is used for turning on led
- `LAMP_OFF` is used for turning off led
- `LOGOUT` is used for logging out from voice command

We can draw our voice command machine states, shown in the following figure:

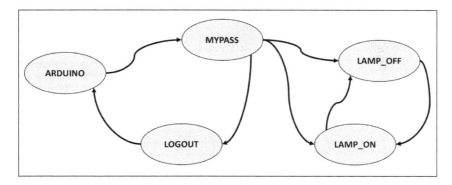

Arduino will start to receive voice command after received the ARDUINO voice command. After that, user will be challenged to send MYPASS voice command. MYPASS state represents be a password. After MYPASS voice command is correct, use can turn on lamp via LAMP_ON and turn off lamp via LAMP_OFF. In addition, user can log out from turn on/off lamp using LOGOUT.

How to build?

After connected Arduino to EasyVR Commander tool (make sure **MODE JUMPER** already set on **PC**), you should see the following figure:

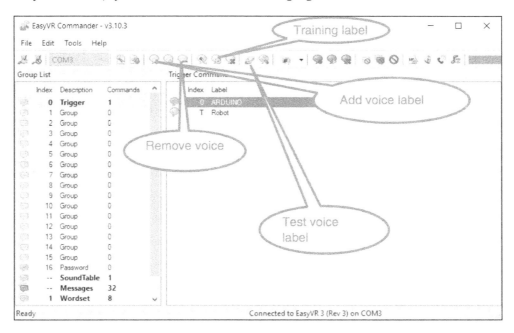

Firstly, we create ARDUINO voice command. Select group 0 (Trigger) on **Group List** pane. Click the add voice label icon (see the preceding figure). Set ARDUINO as label name.

Furthermore, we should train and test our voice command. Select ARDUINO label and then click training label icon. You should get a dialog, shown in the following figure:

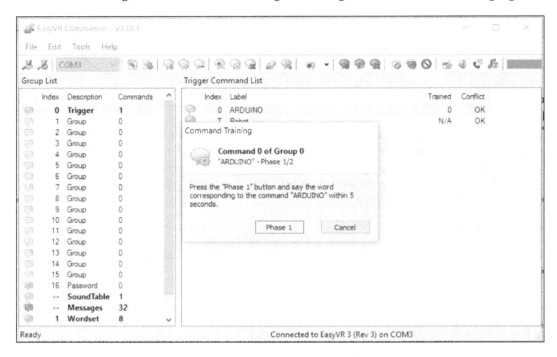

The program provides two trainings. Click **Phase 1** and say something, for instance, ARDUINO. This program will record our voice. Try again for the second training for ARDUINO label.

Now you can test our voice command. EasyVR voice command can only detect voice command in single group so if you want to test our voice command on group 0, you should click **Trigger** (index 0 or group 0).

After that, click test voice label icon. You should see a dialog **Speak now...**, shown in the following figure:

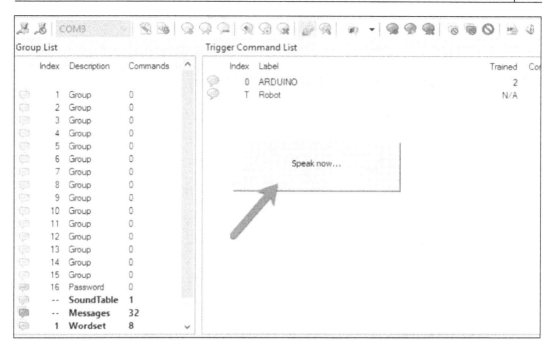

Try to say a voice for ARDUINO label. If detected, the program will show a highlight on your label.

This is a single cycle for building voice command. Now you do the remain voice commands:

- MYPASS label on Password group (index 16)
- LAMP_ON label on Group 1 (index 1)
- LAMP_OFF label on Group 1 (index 1)
- LOGOUT label on Group 1 (index 1)

You start to create a new label, train the label and then test the label.

Now we can generate codes from our defined labels. You can click menu **File | Generate Code** on EasyVR Commander tool. You should see sketch code file (*.ino file). We will modify the sketch program on the next section.

If done, disconnect your Arduino from EasyVR commander tool. We will continue to write a sketch program.

Wiring your voice command board

In my implementation, I use a LED. You can use the real lamp with relay module. Connect LED to digital pin 8 through resistor 330 Ohm. The following is my wiring for this demo.

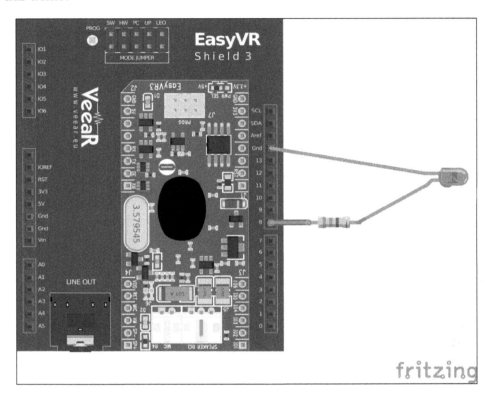

Change **MODE JUMPER** into **SW** mode on EasyVR shield 3 so we can communicate with our Arduino and EasyVR shield 3.

Writing sketch program

We already obtained a skeleton sketch program. Now we modify our program. The following is my modified program:

```
#include "Arduino.h"
#if !defined(SERIAL_PORT_MONITOR)
  #error "Arduino version not supported. Please update your IDE to
  the latest version."
#endif
```

```
#if defined(SERIAL_PORT_USBVIRTUAL)
  // Shield Jumper on HW (for Leonardo and Due)
  #define port SERIAL_PORT_HARDWARE
  #define pcSerial SERIAL_PORT_USBVIRTUAL
#else
  // Shield Jumper on SW (using pins 12/13 or 8/9 as RX/TX)
  #include "SoftwareSerial.h"
  SoftwareSerial port(12, 13);
  #define pcSerial SERIAL_PORT_MONITOR
#endif

#include "EasyVR.h"

EasyVR easyvr(port);

//Groups and Commands
enum Groups
{
  GROUP_0  = 0,
  GROUP_1  = 1,
  GROUP_16 = 16,
};

enum Group0
{
  G0_ARDUINO = 0,
};

enum Group1
{
  G1_LAMP_ON = 0,
  G1_LAMP_OFF = 1,
  G1_LOGOUT = 2,
};

enum Group16
{
  G16_MYPASS = 0,
};


int8_t group, idx;
int myled = 8;
```

```
void setup()
{
  // setup PC serial port
  pcSerial.begin(9600);

  pinMode(myled, OUTPUT);

  // bridge mode?
  int mode = easyvr.bridgeRequested(pcSerial);
  switch (mode)
  {
  case EasyVR::BRIDGE_NONE:
    // setup EasyVR serial port
    port.begin(9600);
    // run normally
    pcSerial.println(F("---"));
    pcSerial.println(F("Bridge not started!"));
    break;

  case EasyVR::BRIDGE_NORMAL:
    // setup EasyVR serial port (low speed)
    port.begin(9600);
    // soft-connect the two serial ports (PC and EasyVR)
    easyvr.bridgeLoop(pcSerial);
    // resume normally if aborted
    pcSerial.println(F("---"));
    pcSerial.println(F("Bridge connection aborted!"));
    break;

  case EasyVR::BRIDGE_BOOT:
    // setup EasyVR serial port (high speed)
    port.begin(115200);
    // soft-connect the two serial ports (PC and EasyVR)
    easyvr.bridgeLoop(pcSerial);
    // resume normally if aborted
    pcSerial.println(F("---"));
    pcSerial.println(F("Bridge connection aborted!"));
    break;
  }

  while (!easyvr.detect())
  {
    Serial.println("EasyVR not detected!");
    delay(1000);
```

```
  }

  easyvr.setPinOutput(EasyVR::IO1, LOW);
  Serial.println("EasyVR detected!");
  easyvr.setTimeout(5);
  easyvr.setLanguage(0);

  group = EasyVR::TRIGGER; //<-- start group (customize)
}

void action();

void loop()
{
  if (easyvr.getID() < EasyVR::EASYVR3)
    easyvr.setPinOutput(EasyVR::IO1, HIGH); // LED on (listening)

  Serial.print("Say username ");
  Serial.println(group);
  easyvr.recognizeCommand(group);

  do
  {
    // can do some processing while waiting for a spoken command
  }
  while (!easyvr.hasFinished());

  if (easyvr.getID() < EasyVR::EASYVR3)
    easyvr.setPinOutput(EasyVR::IO1, LOW); // LED off

  idx = easyvr.getWord();
  if (idx >= 0)
  {
    // built-in trigger (ROBOT)
    // group = GROUP_X; <-- jump to another group X
    //group = GROUP_16;
    return;
  }
  idx = easyvr.getCommand();
  if (idx >= 0)
  {
    // print debug message
    uint8_t train = 0;
    char name[32];
```

```
      Serial.print("Command: ");
      Serial.print(idx);
      if (easyvr.dumpCommand(group, idx, name, train))
      {
        Serial.print(" = ");
        Serial.println(name);
      }
      else
        Serial.println();
      // beep
      easyvr.playSound(0, EasyVR::VOL_FULL);
      // perform some action
      action();
    }
    else // errors or timeout
    {
      if (easyvr.isTimeout())
        Serial.println("Timed out, try again...");
      int16_t err = easyvr.getError();
      if (err >= 0)
      {
        Serial.print("Error ");
        Serial.println(err, HEX);
      }
    }
}

void action()
{
    switch (group)
    {
    case GROUP_0:
      switch (idx)
      {
      case G0_ARDUINO:
        // write your action code here
        Serial.println("Please say password");
        group = GROUP_16;
        break;
      }
      break;
    case GROUP_1:
      switch (idx)
      {
```

```
      case G1_LAMP_ON:
        digitalWrite(myled, HIGH);
        Serial.println("LAMP ON");
        break;
      case G1_LAMP_OFF:
        digitalWrite(myled, LOW);
        Serial.println("LAMP OFF");
        break;
      case G1_LOGOUT:
        group = EasyVR::TRIGGER;
        Serial.println("Logout");
        break;
      }
      break;
    case GROUP_16:
      switch (idx)
      {
      case G16_MYPASS:
        // write your action code here
        Serial.println("OK.Now I'm waiting your command");
        group = GROUP_1;
        break;
      }
      break;
    }
}
```

This program is based on our machine state.

 Remember EasyVR can recognize voices on active group

Save this program and then upload sketch program into Arduino board.

Testing

Now you can test the program. Starting to say a voice for ARDUINO label. Next, say voice for the MYPASS label.

After that, you can turn on LED by saying voice for the LAMP_ON label. Otherwise, say voice for the LAMP_OFF label to turn off.

To stop all commands related to LEDs, you say voice for the LOGOUT label. After that, Arduino only wait voice for the ARDUINO label.

Make your IoT board speak

Making your IoT board speak is interesting. Imagine your board give a voice notification about environment information such as temperature, humidity and so on. This happens if we implement speech module especially about Text-To-Speech module.

In this demo, we use Emic 2 for Text-To-Speech module and Arduino Uno R3 board. You can get it on Sparkfun store, https://www.sparkfun.com/products/11711.

Let's start.

Setting up

We use EMIC2 library to communicate between Arduino Sketch and EMIC 2 module. This library can found on https://github.com/pAIgn10/EMIC2. You can download and put it on Arduino library folder.

Now you can write sketch program using Arduino IDE.

Wiring

Connecting EMIC 2 module into Arduino board is easy. The following is our wiring:

- Connect EMIC2 **5V** to Arduino **5V**
- Connect EMIC2 **GND** to Arduino **GND**
- Connect EMIC2 **SOUT** to Arduino digital pin **9**
- Connect EMIC2 **SIN** to Arduino digital pin **8**
- Connect EMIC2 **SP-** to speaker **-**
- Connect EMIC2 **SP+** to speaker **+**

The following is a sample of our demo wiring:

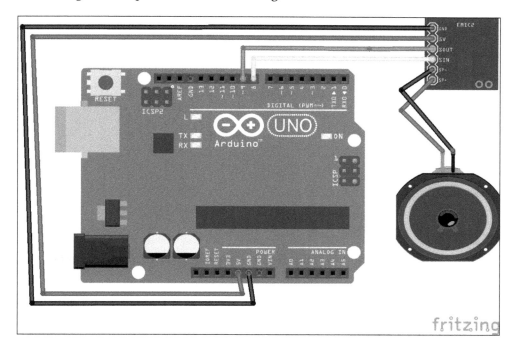

Writing sketch program

We can use `emic.speak()` from the `EMIC2` library to implement Text-To-Speech program. For testing, we build a simple program to say **Hello Arduino** and **I am waiting your command** words.

Write the following sketch program:

```
#include <SoftwareSerial.h>
#include "EMIC2.h"

// Read here: http://arduino.cc/en/Reference/SoftwareSerial
#define RX_PIN 9  // Connect SOUT Emic 2 module to the RX pin
#define TX_PIN 8  // Connect SIN Emic 2 module to the TX pin

EMIC2 emic;

void setup() {
  emic.begin(RX_PIN, TX_PIN);
  emic.setVoice(8);  // Sets the voice (9 choices: 0 - 8)
```

```
  }

  void loop() {
    // put your main code here, to run repeatedly:
    emic.setVolume(10);
    emic.speak("Hello Arduino");
    emic.resetVolume();
    delay(2000);

    emic.speak("I am waiting your command");
    delay(3000);
  }
```

Save the sketch program as `ArTTSDemo`.

Testing

Compile and upload the sketch program into Arduino board. You should hear voices from speaker.

This is a simple program so you extend this program, for instance, read data from Internet and then Arduino speak those words. You can make Arduino speak about current temperature and humidity.

Make Raspberry Pi speak

On previous section, we already learned how to work with voice modules on IoT board, Arduino. In this section, we will learn how to work with voice processing in software. It means we use a software to process voice.

Raspberry Pi board will be used for example to show how to work with voice processing. I use Raspberry Pi 3 board with Raspbian Jessie OS. You can use the latest Raspbian OS.

Setting up

Some Raspberry Pi models, for instance, Raspberry Pi 3, provide audio output via audio jack. You can see it in the following figure:

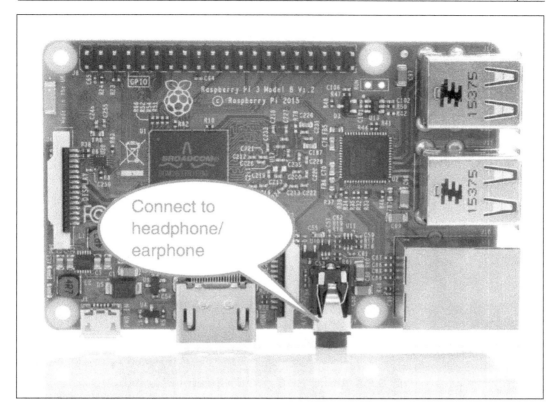

You can connect headphone, earphone or external speaker into Raspberry Pi board. For testing, I use extern speaker using JBL speaker.

In order to work with external speaker, we use configure our Raspberry Pi. You can set it via `rasp-config` on terminal. Type this command.

```
$ sudo raspi-config
```

Then, you should see the `rasp-config` form. Select **9 Advanced Options**:

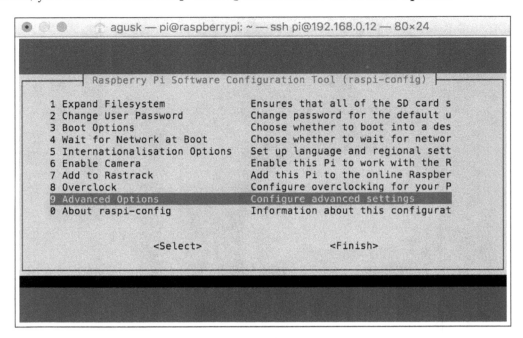

After that, you can select **A9 Audio** to configure Raspberry Pi audio.

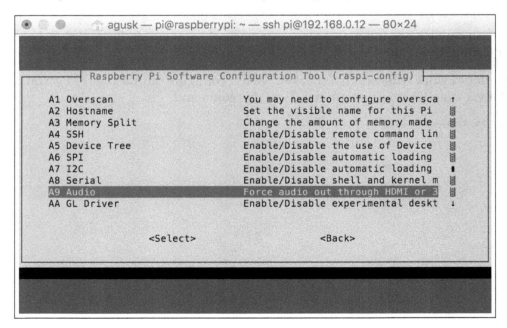

Then, you should see a list of audio output options. Select **1 Force 3.5mm ('headphone') jack**.

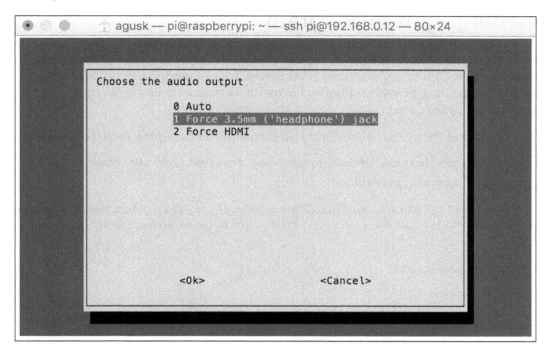

Now your headphone audio output has been configured. The next step is to install audio library. We use festival library, `http://www.cstr.ed.ac.uk/projects/festival/`.

To install festival library on Raspberry Pi, you can type these commands on Raspberry Pi terminal.

```
$ sudo apt-get update
$ sudo apt-get install festival
```

Make sure your Raspberry Pi already connected to Internet network.

Festival library also provides some speech voice model. You can check and install it on `https://packages.debian.org/jessie/festival-voice` for additional voice models.

If done, we can test to generate speech **Good morning!** for testing. You can type this command on terminal.

```
echo "Good morning!" | festival --tts
```

You should hear **Good morning** speech on your own speaker.

Writing Python program

We continue our journey to explore festival library. In this section, we try to write Python program to access festival library so you can customize your program and combine with GPIO programming. Fortunately, we can use the pyfestival library for Python binding of festival library. Further information https://github.com/techiaith/pyfestival.

You can install the pyfestival library on Raspberry Pi by typing these commands:

```
$ sudo apt-get install python python-dev festival festival-dev
$ sudo pip install pyfestival
```

In the pyfestival library, we can call the festival.sayText() function to generate human speech. We can use festival.sayFile() to generate human speech from a file.

Let's write these scripts:

```
import festival

festival.sayText("I am Raspberry Pi")
festival.sayFile("ch05_test_tts.txt")
```

Save these scripts into a file, called ch05_tts.py.

For content of ch05_test_tts.txt file, you can write any content. The following is a content sample:

```
The Raspberry Pi is a series of credit card-sized single-board
computers developed in the United Kingdom by the Raspberry Pi
Foundation to promote the teaching of basic computer science in
schools and developing countries.
```

Save all these texts.

To test our program, you can execute ch05_tts.py using this command.

```
$ python ch05_tts.py
```

You should hear speech voices from a speaker or headphone.

What's next?

This is a simple program but you extend this program by combining with sensor, actuator or electronics component. For instance, if your press a push button on Raspberry Pi, a program in Raspberry Pi will say something.

You also integrate with voice command so your IoT board like Raspberry Pi can communicate with you through voice.

Summary

We have learned some basic sound and voice processing. We also explore several sound and speech modules to integrate into your IoT project. We built a program to read sound intensity level at the first. Then, we build programs with utilizing EasyVR and EMIC 2 modules for voice commander and Text-To-Speech program. The last topic, we make our Raspberry Pi board speak something.

The next chapter we will learn how to integrate our IoT project with cloud technology as back-end computing center.

References

The following is a list of recommend papers, books, and websites you can learn more about the topics in this chapter.

1. Juang, B. H.; Rabiner, Lawrence R. *Automatic speech recognition–a brief history of the technology development.* http://www.ece.ucsb.edu/faculty/Rabiner/ece259/Reprints/354_LALI-ASRHistory-final-10-8.pdf.

2. Benesty, Jacob; Sondhi, M. M.; Huang, Yiteng. Springer Handbook of Speech Processing. Springer Science & Business Media.2008.

3. Wu Chou, Biing-Hwang Juang. Pattern Recognition in Speech and Language Processing. CRC Press, 2003.

6
Building Data Science-based Cloud for IoT Projects

In this chapter, we will explore how to apply cloud platforms on IoT projects. Backend infrastructure for our IoT projects is important. By distributing IoT boards on some location with different countries needs more attention in acquiring sensor data. Cloud-based platforms including data science services are key to scaling your IoT projects.

We will explore the following topics:

- Introducing cloud technology
- Introducing cloud-based data science
- Connecting an IoT board to cloud-based servers
- Building a data science-based cloud
- Making an IoT application with a data science-based cloud

Introduce cloud technology

Cloud technology means moving your local computing and data to other servers over an Internet network. Investing huge infrastructure is very expensive unless you know your risk.

In general, cloud technology provides dynamic infrastructure, so your system does not need to stop if you want to upgrade your infrastructure. There are three terms in cloud technology: SaaS, PaaS and IaaS.

SaaS, or Software as a Service, is the most familiar form of cloud service for consumers. SaaS moves the task of managing software and its deployment to third-party services. Examples of SaaS include DropBox, Google Apps, and other storage solutions.

PaaS, or Platform as a Service, provides a platform on which software can be developed and deployed. Customers focus their business. They can select which platform fits on their business without thinking about network infrastructure and servers. Examples of PaaS include Heroku, Google App Engine, and Red Hat's OpenShift.

IaaS, or Infrastructure as a Service, offers cloud servers and their associated resources via dashboard and/or API. This service is useful if you don't want to manage your assets or don't want to invest a data center place. IaaS usually provides a flexible cloud-computing model and allows for automated deployment of servers, processing power, storage, and networking.

Some cloud providers, such as AWS IoT and Azure IoT, provide SDK/API to enable your IoT board to connect to their resources. You can manage and analyze sensor data inside cloud servers:

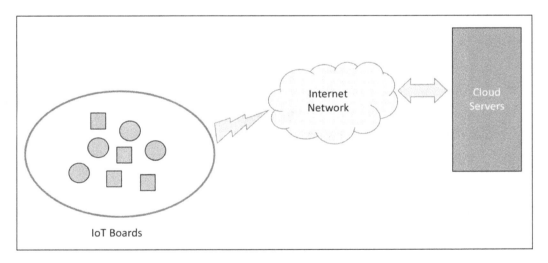

Introducing cloud-based data science

In data science, we talk about regression, classification, and prediction. This type of computing needs huge resources to perform data science tasks.

Data science-based cloud is one solution to address resource issues. You can optimize resources to perform classification and prediction. A high availability feature is usually offered by cloud providers.

Companies such as Microsoft, Amazon, and Google have already implemented data science servers. We can use R or Python to write programs for data science. They will take care of pre- and post-processing on our sensor data.

An example of a cloud-based machine-learning dashboard can be seen in the following screenshot. This is a Microsoft Azure machine-learning dashboard:

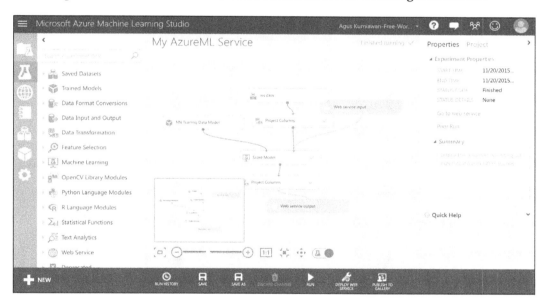

Connecting IoT boards to cloud-based server

Connecting to a cloud-based server means your IoT boards have networking capabilities, which are used to connect to a remote server. You can use either an Ethernet module or a wireless module on IoT boards.

There are many platforms for cloud-based servers you can integrate with IoT boards. In this section, we will explore some cloud-based server platforms.

Let's explore!

Microsoft Azure IoT

Microsoft started its cloud service with Microsoft Azure, which provides many options for solving your IT problems. Microsoft provides the Azure portal to manage your cloud services. The Azure portal is shown in the following screenshot:

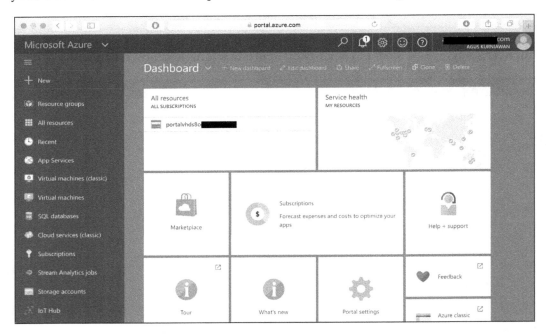

For further information about Microsoft Azure, I recommend you visit https://azure.microsoft.com/. I don't explain all Microsoft Azure services in this book. I will explain Azure IoT in the following section.

Amazon AWS IoT

Amazon already provides cloud technology, called Amazon AWS. Now Amazon AWS also provides an IoT solution. Your board can connect, push, and pull data to/ from AWS.

In general, AWS IoT architecture can be described by the following figure:

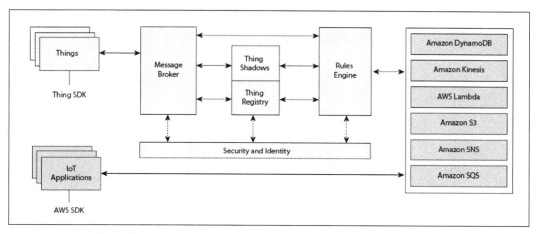

Image source: http://docs.aws.amazon.com/iot/latest/developerguide/aws-iot-how-it-works.html

You can see that our boards connect to AWS IoT through Message Broker. Some rules can be applied to filter your data. On backend site, Amazon AWS has many services to manage your data, such as Amazon DynamoDB, Kinesis, AWS Lambda, and Amazon S3. These features can optimize our IoT data processing.

Further information about how AWS IoT works can be found at `http://docs.aws.amazon.com/iot/latest/developerguide/aws-iot-how-it-works.html`.

Arduino Cloud

To connect your Arduino boards to a cloud-based server, Arduino (arduino.cc) provides a free cloud-based server. You can visit the official site at `https://cloud.arduino.cc/`. To access this cloud, you should register to that portal:

Currently, Arduino Cloud provides an MQTT broker, which enable your Arduino boards to send messages from one board to another.

If you want to work with Arduino Cloud, you should have specific network modules or Arduino board models. The following is a list of network modules and boards that are compatible with Arduino Cloud:

- Arduino/Genuino Yún Shield
- Arduino/Genuino MKR1000
- WiFi Shield 101

For this demo, I use an Arduino MKR1000 board, `https://www.arduino.cc/en/Main/ArduinoMKR1000`, for development, which will be connected to Arduino Cloud.

Setting up Arduino Cloud

After registered with the Arduino Cloud website, we can access Arduino Cloud from our Arduino board. The first step is to register our board with Arduino Cloud.

You can register your Arduino board using this link, `https://cloud.arduino.cc/cloud/getting-started`, or you can visit their website at `https://cloud.arduino.cc/cloud` to register a new device. Then, you can click the **NEW THING** button, which will bring up the screen shown in the following screenshot:

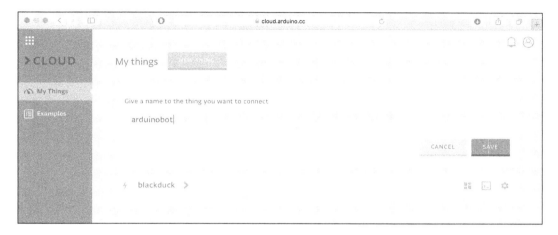

Type in a name of your Arduino board, for instance, `arduinobot`. Once done, click on the **SAVE** button to save your board's name.

You will see your IoT board name shown on the Arduino Cloud dashboard:

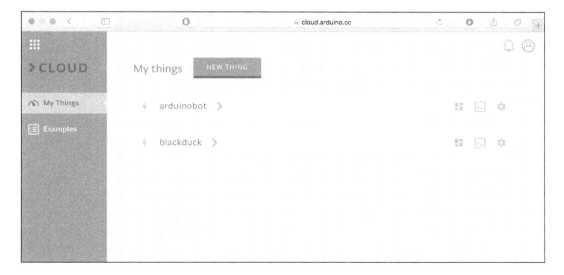

Now we should define some sensor properties for our demo. In our scenario, we create two properties: Temperature and Humidity. These properties will be used for our Arduino board to push and pull sensor data.

On your registered board, click on the left-hand icon to show your board properties. You should see a web form, as shown in the following screenshot:

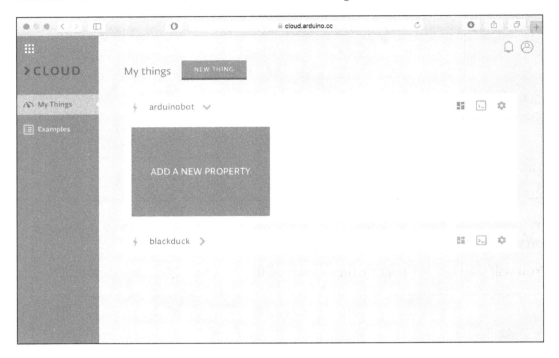

Click the **ADD A NEW PROPERTY** button. Then, enter the following values:

- **Name**: Humidity
- **Type**: Float
- **Policy**: Update when the value changes

Once completed, click the **SAVE** button to save your board properties:

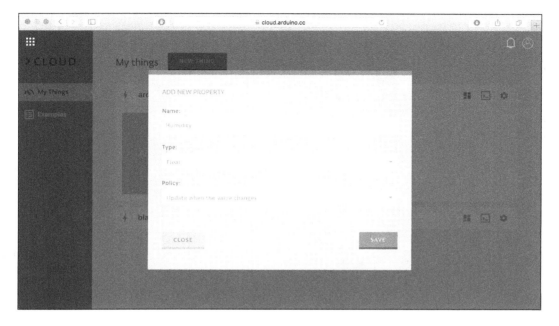

Do the same thing for our second board properties, using the following settings:

- **Name**: Temperature
- **Type**: Float
- **Policy**: Update when the value changes

Now you should see two created board properties, as shown in the following screenshot:

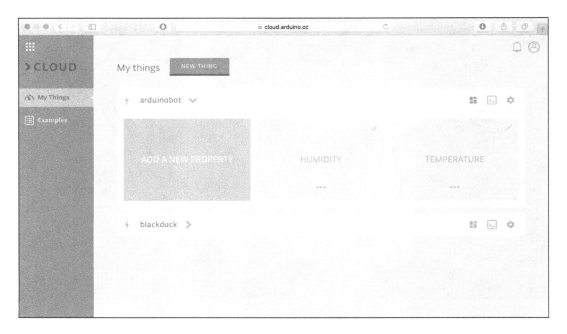

The two properties of Arduino Cloud on our Arduino board will be used as a data target. I will explain how to access these properties in the following section.

Wiring for demo

We will use a DHT-22 sensor to obtain temperature and humidity data. We have learned how to use DHT-22 on our board.

In this case, we connect our DHT-22 sensor module to our Arduino MKR1000. You can do the wiring as follows:

- VDD (pin 1) is connected to the VCC (3.3V) pin on Arduino
- SIG (pin 2) is connected to digital pin 8 on Arduino
- GND (pin 4) is connected to GND on Arduino

You can see this wiring in the following figure:

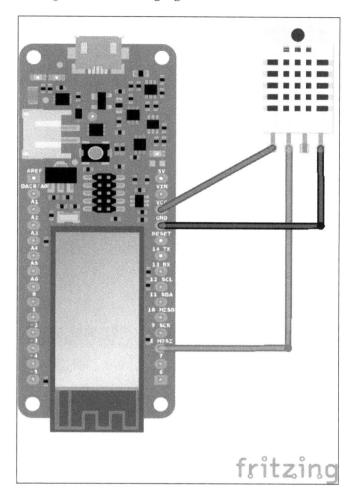

Adding Arduino Cloud library

Arduino Cloud provides an MQTT protocol to push and pull data. On the Arduino platform, we can use the ArduinoCloud library to access the Arduino Cloud server. This library is an open source library. You can review this library at https://github.com/arduino-libraries/ArduinoCloud.

To install `ArduinoCloud`, we use Arduino IDE. Click the menu **Sketch | Include Library | Manage Libraries**. Once done, you should see a dialog, Library Manager, which is shown in the following screenshot:

Type `arduinocloud` on text so you see the `ArduinoCloud` library. Click the **Install** button on the bottom-right.

Once installation is complete, you are ready to develop your Sketch program.

Updating Arduino Cloud web SSL certificate

If you use an Arduino MKR1000 or an Arduino board with a WiFi101 shield, you should update the SSL certificate for the Arduino Cloud website (arduino.cc).

Download the latest firmware updater tool from `https://github.com/arduino-libraries/WiFi101-FirmwareUpdater/releases`.

Now you can open Arduino IDE. Open the `FirmwareUpdater` program by clicking the menu **File | Examples | WiFi101 | FirmwareUpdater** so you should the following program Sketch.

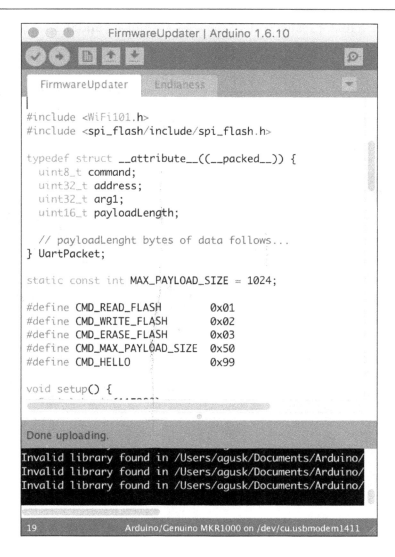

Select the Arduino board target and its port on Arduino IDE. Then compile and upload this program to your Arduino board.

On the computer to which your Arduino board is attached, you can also run the WINC1500 SSL Certificate updater. Type the following command:

```
$ ./winc1500-uploader-gui
```

You should see a dialog, called WINC1500 SSL Certificate updater, which is shown in the following screenshot:

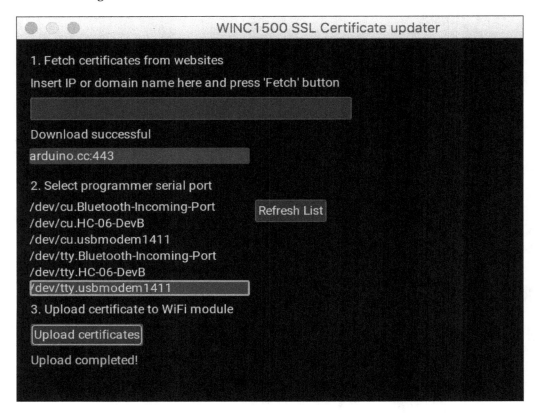

Then you should perform the following steps:

1. Type `arduino.cc` in the text field of step 1 (Fetch certificates from websites).
2. Click the **Fetch** button to download the SSL certificate from arduino.cc.
3. In step 2, you select an Arduino port.
4. Once done, click the **Update certificates** button to flash the SSL certificate onto your Arduino board.

Now your WINC1500 firmware has an updated SSL certificate for the Arduino.cc website.

Writing program for Arduino Cloud

The next step is to write a Sketch program for our demo. Basically, we can use the sample code from our registered board on Arduino Cloud. You just click the middle icon on your registered board. You should see some skeleton code, as shown in the following screenshot:

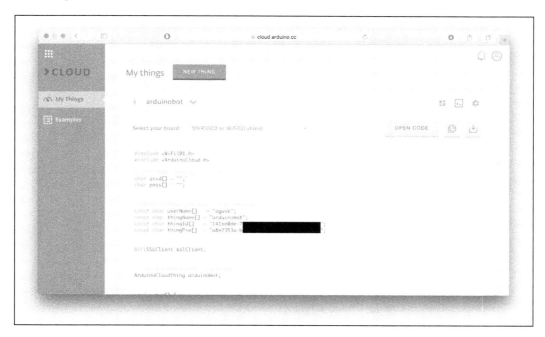

Copy and paste this Sketch program into Arduino IDE.

Next, we modify this Sketch program with integrating DHT-22 sensor. The program will read temperature and humidity via the DHT-22. We will then send the sensor data to Arduino Cloud.

Write the complete code as follows:

```
#include <WiFi101.h>
#include <ArduinoCloud.h>
#include "DHT.h"

/////// Wifi Settings //////
char ssid[] = "<your_ssid>";
char pass[] = "<your_ssid_password";
```

```
// Arduino Cloud settings and credentials
const char userName[]  = "<your_thing_username>";
const char thingName[] = "<your_thins_name>";
const char thingId[]   = "<your_thing_id>";
const char thingPsw[]  = "<your_thing_password>";


WiFiSSLClient sslClient;


// build a new object "arduinobot"
ArduinoCloudThing arduinobot;


// define DHT22
#define DHTTYPE DHT22
// define pin on DHT22
#define DHTPIN 8

DHT dht(DHTPIN, DHTTYPE);

void setup() {
  Serial.begin (9600);

  dht.begin();

  // attempt to connect to WiFi network:
  Serial.print("Attempting to connect to WPA SSID: ");
  Serial.println(ssid);

  while (WiFi.begin(ssid, pass) != WL_CONNECTED) {
    // unsuccessful, retry in 4 seconds
    Serial.print("failed ... ");
    delay(4000);
    Serial.print("retrying ... ");
  }
  Serial.println("connected to wifi");
```

```
  arduinobot.begin(thingName, userName, thingId, thingPsw, sslClient);
  arduinobot.enableDebug();

  // define the properties
  arduinobot.addProperty("Humidity", FLOAT, R);
  arduinobot.addProperty("Temperature", FLOAT, R);
}

void loop() {

  arduinobot.poll();

  delay(2000);

  // Reading temperature or humidity takes about 250 milliseconds!
  // Sensor readings may also be up to 2 seconds 'old' (its a very
slow sensor)
  float h = dht.readHumidity();
  // Read temperature as Celsius (the default)
  float t = dht.readTemperature();


  // Check if any reads failed and exit early (to try again).
  if (isnan(h) || isnan(t)) {
    Serial.println("Failed to read from DHT sensor!");
    return;
  }

  arduinobot.writeProperty("Temperature", t);
  arduinobot.writeProperty("Humidity", h);
  delay(1000);
}
```

Modify the values for Wi-Fi and Arduino Cloud. Once done, save this Sketch program as ch06_01.

Now compile and upload this program to your Arduino board.

Open the Serial Monitor tool from Arduino IDE. You should see the program connect to Wi-Fi and then sense temperature and humidity through the DHT-22. After it has finished reading the sensor data, the program will send the data to Arduino Cloud.

The following is a sample of the program output on my Serial monitor tool:

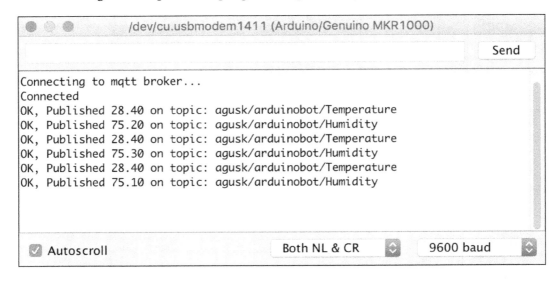

Open the Arduino Cloud website and navigate to your registered Arduino board. You should see values for temperature and humidity:

How does it work? This program works very simply. Using the setup() function, we activate the serial port and DHT-22 module. Then, try to connect to your Wi-Fi:

```
Serial.begin (9600);
dht.begin();


while (WiFi.begin(ssid, pass) != WL_CONNECTED) {

    // unsuccessful, retry in 4 seconds

    Serial.print("failed ... ");

    delay(4000);

    Serial.print("retrying ... ");

}
```

We also call the ArduinoCloud library and define the board properties:

```
arduinobot.begin(thingName, userName, thingId, thingPsw,
sslClient);arduinobot.enableDebug();

// define the properties
arduinobot.addProperty("Humidity", FLOAT, R);
```

Using the loop() function, we perform poll() to Arduino Cloud:

```
arduinobot.poll();
delay(2000);
```

Then, we take temperature and humidity readings via the DHT-22 sensor. After that, we send them to Arduino Cloud:

```
float h = dht.readHumidity();
float t = dht.readTemperature();
if (isnan(h) || isnan(t)) {
    Serial.println("Failed to read from DHT sensor!");
    return;
}

arduinobot.writeProperty("Temperature", t);
arduinobot.writeProperty("Humidity", h);
delay(1000);
```

Working with Microsoft Azure IoT Hub

Azure IoT Hub offers reliable device-to-cloud and cloud-to-device hyper-scale messaging, enables secure communications using per-device security credentials and access control, and includes device libraries for the most popular languages and platforms.

Various IoT boards can be connected to Azure IoT Hub. You can check if your board can connect or not by visiting `https://azure.microsoft.com/en-us/develop/iot/get-started/`.

In this section, we will try to access Microsoft Azure IoT Hub from our Raspberry Pi or desktop. You can use any board if you want to test. Let's start!

Setting up Microsoft Azure IoT Hub

To set up Microsoft Azure IoT Hub, you should have an active subscription on Microsoft Azure. Microsoft also provides a trial account.

Open a browser and navigate to `https://portal.azure.com/` to open Microsoft Azure. In the left-hand menu, find IoT Hub so you can see the IoT Hub dashboard, which is shown in the following screenshot:

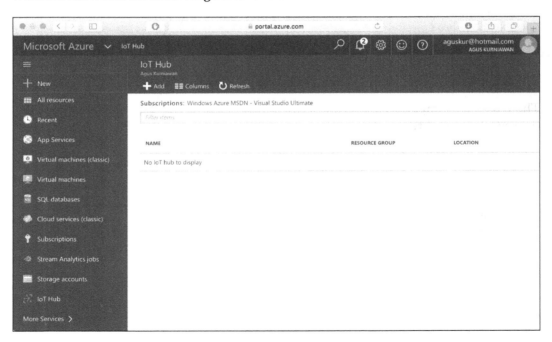

On the IoT Hub dashboard, you can click **+ Add** to add a new IoT hub. You should then see a form, as shown in the following screenshot:

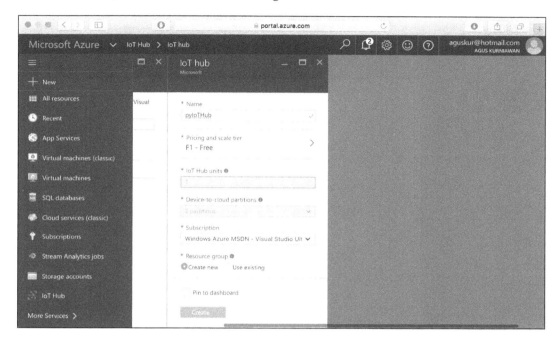

Fill all the required fields, including pricing and scale tier. At the time of writing, a free option is available, called *F1*.

Once finished, click the **Create** button:

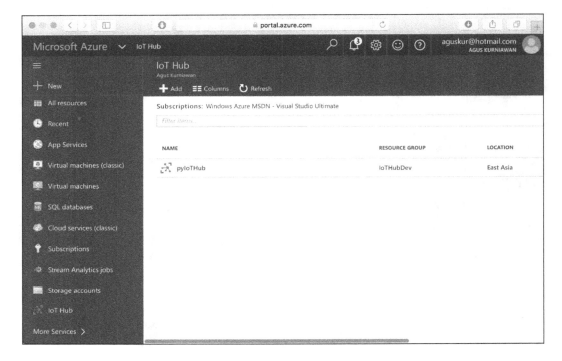

Microsoft Azure IoT Hub will create the new hub for you. It may take some time for Microsoft Azure to complete this task.

Next, once your new Azure IoT hub is created, you're ready to customize it.

Registering IoT device

In order to use your IoT board with Microsoft Azure IoT Hub, you should register your board. After that, you can obtain access credentials.

There are two options for registering an IoT device.

Open your **Microsoft Azure | IoT Hub | Settings**. You should see a list of menus, as shown in the following screenshot:

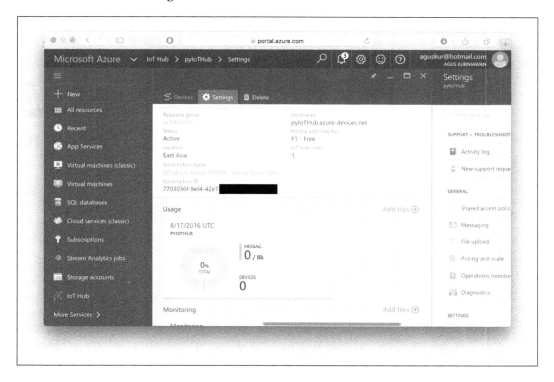

Click the menu **Shared** access policies and should see a list of access policies, as shown in the following screenshot:

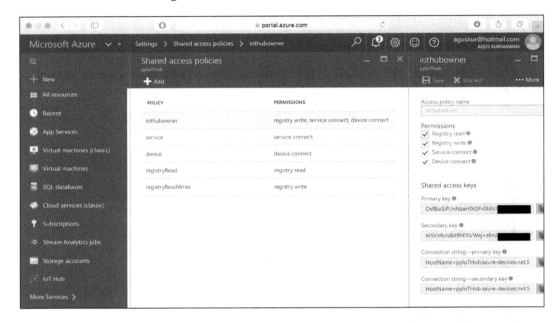

Click the `iothubowner` policy. You should see shared access keys. Copy a value of `Connection string - primary key`.

The connection string will be used to add a new IoT board to access Azure IoT. Currently, we can do this in two ways: `iothub-explorer` or Device explorer tools.

The `iothub-explorer` tool is a command-line tool-based Node.js, which can run any platform. The Device Explorer tool is a GUI tool-based Windows platform, so this tool only runs on Windows OS.

For further information about how to work with the `iothub-explorer` tool, I recommend you read this article, https://github.com/Azure/azure-iot-sdks/blob/master/tools/iothub-explorer/readme.md.

In this section, I will share how to use the Device Explorer tool on Windows 10 to register a new IoT board.

You can download and install the setup file for the Device Explorer tool from `https://github.com/Azure/azure-iot-sdks/releases`. Once run, paste the connection string to the Configuration tab, which already copied to Connection Information field from this tool. You can see this in the following screenshot:

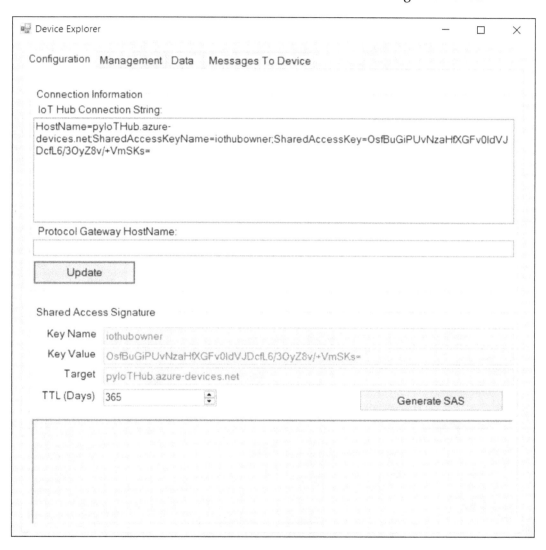

After you have pasted your Azure IoT Hub connection string, click the **Update** button. If successful, click on the **Management** tab, which is shown in the following screenshot:

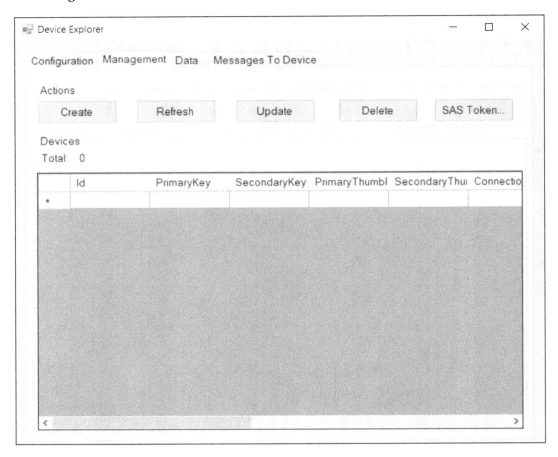

To add a new IoT device, click the **Create** button. You will get a dialog, as shown in the following screenshot:

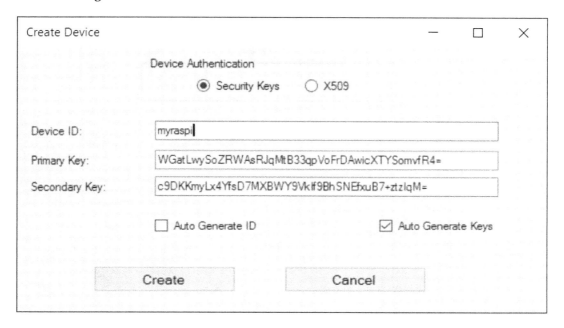

Type in a name for your device, and then click the **Create** button. If successful, you should see your device on the **Device Explorer** tool under the **Management** tab.

Next, we should get a connection string from our IoT device. Right-click on your device and you should see a context menu:

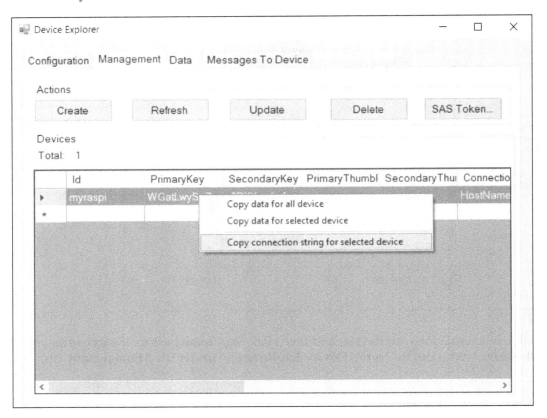

Select **Copy connection string for selected device**. Then, paste it into any text editor. This value will be used in our program.

I will explain it in the following section.

Writing program

We will use Python to write a program for Azure IoT Hub. For testing purposes, I use a Raspberry Pi with Raspbian OS.

You can download and install Azure IoT SDK for your platform from `https://github.com/Azure/azure-iot-sdks`. Before installed from source code, we should increase our swap file configuration on Raspbian.

Open Terminal and type the following command:

```
$ sudo nano /etc/dphys-swapfile
```

Locate the following line:

```
CONF_SWAPSIZE=100
```

Then, change it to the following:

```
CONF_SWAPSIZE=1024
```

Once done, reboot a swap file service or reboot Raspbian.

The next step is to install SDK for Azure IoT from source code, `https://github.com/Azure/azure-iot-sdks.git`. First, we install Azure IoT SDK for C because the Python library for Azure IoT is needed for Python binding.

Type the following commands in your Raspberry Pi Terminal:

```
$ sudo apt-get update
$ git clone --recursive https://github.com/Azure/azure-iot-sdks.git
$ cd azure-iot-sdks/c/build_all/linux/
$ ./setup.sh
$ ./build.sh
```

Once complete, you should install for Python library. Navigate to `/python/build_all/linux/` and type the following commands:

```
$ cd ../../../
$ cd python/build_all/linux/
$ ./setup.sh
$ ./build.sh
```

After installation is complete, we can find the library file, `iothub_client.so`, in the `<sdk_azure_iot_hub>/python/device/samples/` folder. Copy this file to a folder you're working with. You can also put it on Python library path on Raspberry Pi.

For our demo, we are going to write a program to access Azure IoT. I have modified a Python sample program from `https://github.com/Azure/azure-iot-sdks`. In this case, we will send temperature and humidity sensor data to Azure IoT Hub.

Write the following scripts:

```python
#!/usr/bin/env python

import random
import time
import sys
import iothub_client
from iothub_client import *


# messageTimeout - the maximum time in milliseconds until a message
times out.
message_timeout = 10000

receive_context = 0
avg_temperature = 0
avg_humidity = 0
message_count = 3
received_count = 0

# global counters
receive_callbacks = 0
send_callbacks = 0

# MQTT as transport protocol
protocol = IoTHubTransportProvider.MQTT

# String containing Hostname, Device Id & Device Key in the format:
# "HostName=<host_name>;DeviceId=<device_id>;SharedAccessKey=<device_
key>"
connection_string = "[device connection string]"

msg_txt = "{\"deviceId\": \"<device_id>\",\"temperature\":
%.2f,\"humidity\": %.2f}"

# some embedded platforms need certificate information
def set_certificates(iotHubClient):
    from iothub_client_cert import certificates
    try:
```

```
        iotHubClient.set_option("TrustedCerts", certificates)
        print("set_option TrustedCerts successful")
    except IoTHubClientError as e:
        print("set_option TrustedCerts failed (%s)" % e)


def receive_message_callback(message, counter):
    global receive_callbacks
    buffer = message.get_bytearray()
    size = len(buffer)
    print("Received Message [%d]:" % counter)
    print("    Data: <<<%s>>> & Size=%d" % (buffer[:size].
decode('utf-8'), size))
    map_properties = message.properties()
    key_value_pair = map_properties.get_internals()
    print("    Properties: %s" % key_value_pair)
    counter += 1
    receive_callbacks += 1
    print("    Total calls received: %d" % receive_callbacks)
    return IoTHubMessageDispositionResult.ACCEPTED


def send_confirmation_callback(message, result, user_context):
    global send_callbacks
    print(
        "Confirmation[%d] received for message with result = %s" %
        (user_context, result))
    map_properties = message.properties()
    print("    message_id: %s" % message.message_id)
    print("    correlation_id: %s" % message.correlation_id)
    key_value_pair = map_properties.get_internals()
    print("    Properties: %s" % key_value_pair)
    send_callbacks += 1
    print("    Total calls confirmed: %d" % send_callbacks)
```

```python
def iothub_client_init():
    # prepare iothub client
    iotHubClient = IoTHubClient(connection_string, protocol)
    # set the time until a message times out
    iotHubClient.set_option("messageTimeout", message_timeout)
    if iotHubClient.protocol == IoTHubTransportProvider.MQTT:
        iotHubClient.set_option("logtrace", 0)
    iotHubClient.set_message_callback(
        receive_message_callback, receive_context)
    return iotHubClient


def iothub_client_sample_run():

    try:

        iotHubClient = iothub_client_init()

        while True:
            # send a few messages every minute
            print("IoTHubClient sending %d messages" % message_count)

            for i in range(0, message_count):
                msg_txt_formatted = msg_txt % ((random.random() * 4 +
10), (random.random() * 4 + 60))
                # messages can be encoded as string or bytearray
                if (i & 1) == 1:
                    message = IoTHubMessage(bytearray(msg_txt_
formatted, 'utf8'))
                else:
                    message = IoTHubMessage(msg_txt_formatted)
                # optional: assign ids
                message.message_id = "message_%d" % i
                message.correlation_id = "correlation_%d" % i
                # optional: assign properties
                prop_map = message.properties()
                prop_text = "PropMsg_%d" % i
                prop_map.add("Property", prop_text)
                iotHubClient.send_event_async(message, send_
confirmation_callback, i)
```

```
                    print(
                        "IoTHubClient.send_event_async accepted message
    [%d]"
                        " for transmission to IoT Hub." %
                        i)
                # Wait for Commands or exit
                print("IoTHubClient waiting for commands, press Ctrl-C to
    exit")

                n = 0
                while n < 6:
                    status = iotHubClient.get_send_status()
                    print("Send status: %s" % status)
                    time.sleep(10)
                    n += 1

        except IoTHubError as e:
            print("Unexpected error %s from IoTHub" % e)
            return
        except KeyboardInterrupt:
            print("IoTHubClient sample stopped")


    if __name__ == '__main__':
        print('Demo Azure IoT Hub')
        iothub_client_sample_run()
```

Modify a value for the `connection_string` variable and put your device ID in
`<device_id>` of the `msg_txt` variable.

Save these scripts into a file called `ch06_02.py`. Now you can run this program using
the following command:

```
$ python ch06_02.py
```

This program will send temperature and humidity about `message_count` messages.
By default, `message_count` is set to 3.

A sample of the program can be seen in the following screenshot:

```
● ● ●   ⌂  agusk — pi@raspberrypi: ~/Documents/book — ssh pi@192.168.0.12 — 80×28
pi@raspberrypi:~/Documents/book $ python ch06_02.py
Demo Azure IoT Hub
Info: IoT Hub SDK for C, version 1.0.13
IoTHubClient sending 3 messages
IoTHubClient.send_event_async accepted message [0] for transmission to IoT Hub.
IoTHubClient.send_event_async accepted message [1] for transmission to IoT Hub.
IoTHubClient.send_event_async accepted message [2] for transmission to IoT Hub.
IoTHubClient waiting for commands, press Ctrl-C to exit
Send status: BUSY
Confirmation[0] received for message with result = OK
    message_id: message_0
    correlation_id: correlation_0
    Properties: {'Property': 'PropMsg_0'}
    Total calls confirmed: 1
Confirmation[1] received for message with result = OK
    message_id: message_1
    correlation_id: correlation_1
    Properties: {'Property': 'PropMsg_1'}
    Total calls confirmed: 2
Confirmation[2] received for message with result = OK
    message_id: message_2
    correlation_id: correlation_2
    Properties: {'Property': 'PropMsg_2'}
    Total calls confirmed: 3
Send status: IDLE
Send status: IDLE
Send status: IDLE
Send status: IDLE
```

You can see the sent messages using the Device Explorer tool. You can click on the **Data** tab and then click the **Monitor** button to listen to incoming messages from this device. A sample of the tool's output is shown in the following screenshot:

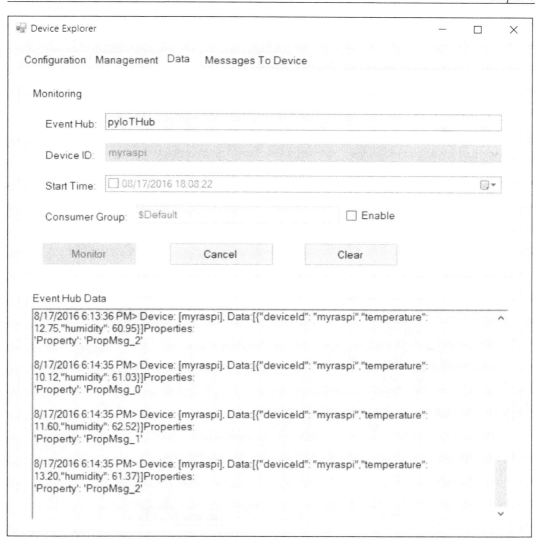

How does it work? This program runs by calling a `iothub_client_sample_run()` function. First, we call the `iothub_client_init()` function to initialize our Azure IoT Hub library. We set MQTT as the transport protocol provider:

```
def iothub_client_init():
    # prepare iothub client
    iotHubClient = IoTHubClient(connection_string, protocol)
    # set the time until a message times out
    iotHubClient.set_option("messageTimeout", message_timeout)
```

```
if iotHubClient.protocol == IoTHubTransportProvider.MQTT:
    iotHubClient.set_option("logtrace", 0)
iotHubClient.set_message_callback(
    receive_message_callback, receive_context)
return iotHubClient
```

After that, we construct sending messages. In this case, I set temperature and humidity values using `random.random()`:

```
msg_txt_formatted = msg_txt % ((random.random() * 4 + 10), (random.
random() * 4 + 60))
# messages can be encoded as string or bytearray
if (i & 1) == 1:
    message = IoTHubMessage(bytearray(msg_txt_formatted, 'utf8'))
else:
    message = IoTHubMessage(msg_txt_formatted)
```

Now we can set message properties and send them to Azure IoT Hub by calling `send_event_async()`:

```
# optional: assign ids
message.message_id = "message_%d" % i
message.correlation_id = "correlation_%d" % i
# optional: assign properties
prop_map = message.properties()
prop_text = "PropMsg_%d" % i
prop_map.add("Property", prop_text)
iotHubClient.send_event_async(message, send_confirmation_callback, i)
```

This program will be executed about *n* times. The value of n is defined as `message_count`.

Building data science-based cloud

After we have acquired data through physical sensor devices, we obtain some data. The next question is, *What do we do with this data?* In this case, we should analyze the data to obtain insight. Machine learning, data science, and data mining are common terms related to data analytics.

Investing in machines to compute machine learning algorithms can be very expensive. One alternative solution is to implement machine learning — or data science-based cloud servers.

Several cloud providers provide data analytics services to manage large amounts of data. It covers various machine learning algorithms. Companies, for instance, Microsoft, Amazon, and Google, offer this service included IoT boards connectivity.

In this section, I will explain how to work with Microsoft Azure Machine Learning. To develop machine learning, Microsoft provides us with Azure ML Studio. You can read about it at `https://studio.azureml.net/`.

For our demo scenario, we use a common problem to classify an iris flower. The dataset is available at `https://archive.ics.uci.edu/ml/datasets/Iris`.

Let's start!

Deploying Azure Machine learning

To deploy Azure Machine Learning, you should have an active subscription for Microsoft Azure. Open a browser and navigate to `https://studio.azureml.net/`.

Azure ML Studio can help you build a machine learning model. It provides various machine-learning algorithms, including pre- and post-processing. I recommend you read the Azure ML documentation at `https://azure.microsoft.com/en-us/documentation/services/machine-learning/`.

The following screenshot shows a machine-learning design form in Azure ML Studio:

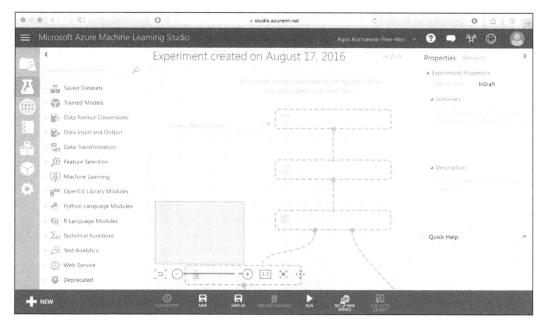

Just click and drag ML components from the toolbox to the design form. For instance, I created a machine learning model for the classification of an iris flower using Neural Network. You can see it in the following screenshot:

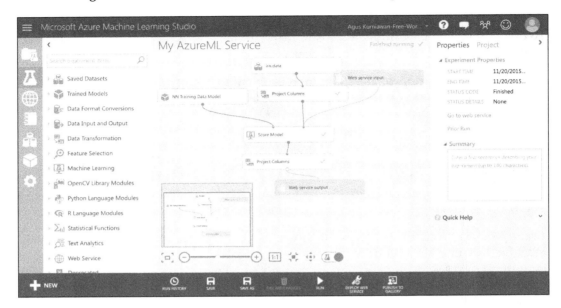

Publishing Azure ML as web service

If you have finished building a machine learning model on Azure ML Studio, you can publish it as a web service. Just map which pinout as web service input and output. After that, you can click **DEPLOY WEB SERVICE** on the bottom menu. You should see the web service dashboard, as shown in the following screenshot:

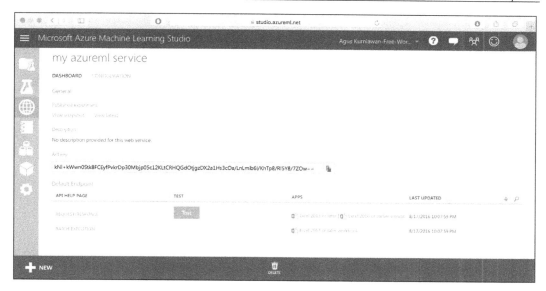

To test, click the **Test** button and you will get a modal dialog, as shown in the following screenshot:

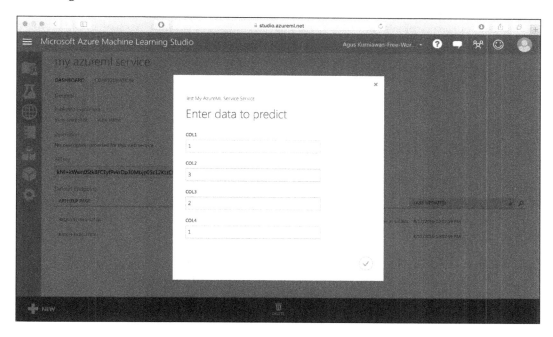

Fill in all the required fields for web service input. Once done, click the button on the bottom-right. You should see the result output on website.

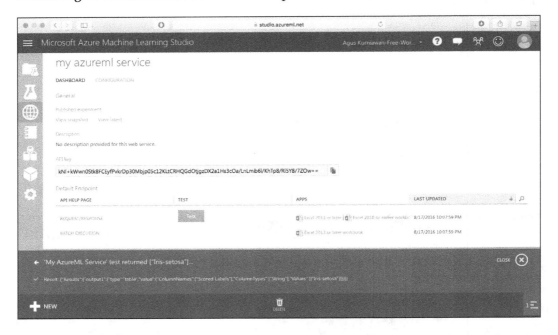

For this scenario, your IoT boards can consume this web service. The board will be used as a sensing node. Computing, such as classification and prediction, can be moved to cloud servers.

Make IoT application with data science-based cloud

Building a complex IoT project is useful by applying cloud servers as back-end. As we know, IoT boards are not usually able to compute complex algorithms due to a lack of resources.

Imagine you have several IoT boards with temperature and humidity sensors deployed at various locations. These boards will sense and send sensor data to servers. The backend servers consist of storage and machine learning servers, which compute and predict data source:

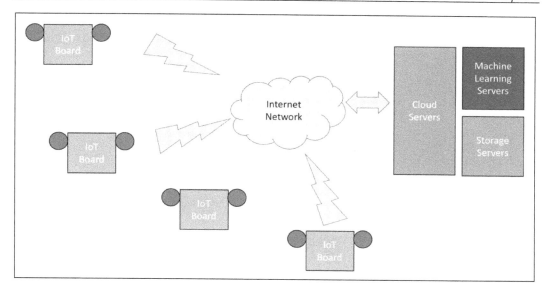

The result of prediction and computation will notify to users. This is only one example of such a scenario. You can apply this architecture to your own problems.

Summary

In this chapter, we have learned some basic cloud technology, which can be applied to IoT projects. We also explored several cloud platforms, such as Arduino Cloud and Microsoft Azure. We built a program to access Arduino Cloud. Then, we built a Python program that interacts with Microsoft Azure IoT. Finally, we made a machine learning model on the Azure Machine Learning platform.

References: The following is a list of recommended papers, books, and websites, where you can learn more about the topics in this chapter:

1. Microsoft Azure IoT Hub, `https://azure.microsoft.com/en-us/services/iot-hub/`.

2. Microsoft Azue Machine Learning, `https://azure.microsoft.com/en-us/services/machine-learning/`.

Index

www.ingramcontent.com/pod-product-compliance
Lightning Source LLC
Chambersburg PA
CBHW060538060326
40690CB00017B/3534